After Seven Wows and time in the Tomb, Jesus Resurrects on the Third Day

For Youth Groups, Jesus Lovers, Church Leaders, Bible Study Groups, and Families eager for a deeper understanding of our Lord Jesus Christ
(Study Guide Included)

Debbie Dunn

FYI - Unless otherwise noted, most Biblical quotes come from either the King James Version (KJV) or the New International Version (NIV) of the Bible APP.

<u>Permissions</u>: This book or any portion thereof may not be reproduced or used in any manner without the publisher's express written permission except for using brief quotations in a book review. For copy permission, please email the author, Debbie Dunn, at moredunntales@yahoo.com. Place, in the subject line: **After Seven Wows and time in the Tomb, Jesus Resurrects on the Third Day**

<u>Disclaimer</u>: The content used in this book is intended for educational and informational purposes only.

ISBN: 9798227878731

Imprint: Independently published. Distributed by Draft 2 Digital

T.R.E.A.T. Tales Presents

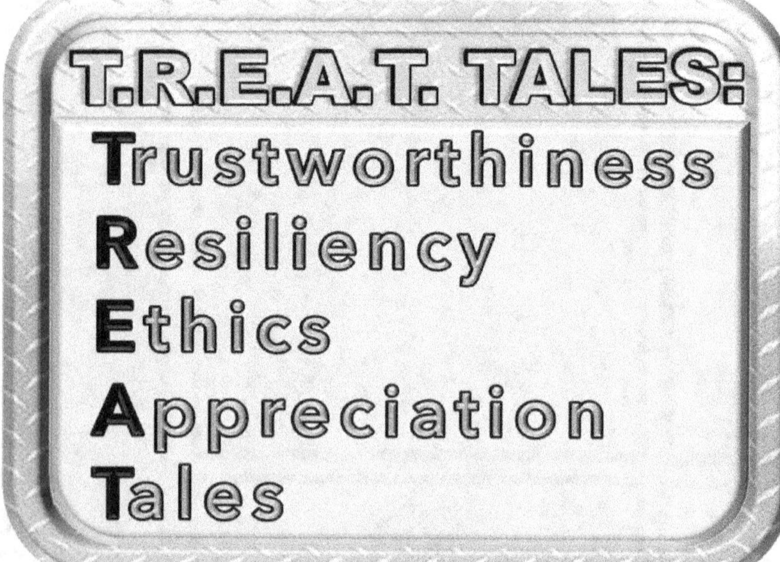

Website: https://bible-books-for-his-glory.com/index.html
Email: moredunntales@yahoo.com

About the Author: Debbie Dunn

Debbie Dunn has been a professional storyteller since 1989. She has also taught at-risk teens, served as an anti-bullying specialist, and taught elementary and middle school. In her retirement years, she indulges her love of our Lord Jesus Christ, nature, traveling, and writing as she pursues learning and exploring more about the Holy Bible.

After Seven Wows and time in the Tomb, Jesus Resurrects on the Third Day *is* a book crafted for youth groups, Jesus lovers, church leaders, Bible study groups, and families. The author, deeply understanding these groups' unique needs and interests, has filled this book with conceptual color illustrations that will resonate with them and has included a study guide for their convenience.

Seven Wows (unanticipated things) occurred right after Jesus died:
❶ Jesus died on command around 3 PM on Friday, 30 AD.
❷ The 60-foot-tall veil tore in the temple from top to bottom.
❸ An Earthquake followed.
❹ Some tombs opened, and these holy people walked around Jerusalem after Jesus' resurrection.
❺ A Roman centurion concluded Jesus was the Son of God.
❻ Followers of Jesus grieved and smote their chests when they saw the mangled appearance of Jesus' tortured body.
❼ To ascertain that Jesus was dead, a Roman soldier pierced His side with a spear but did not break His legs.

Other parts of this book include:
● Timeline from Adam to the Flood to King David to Jesus to Today.
● Pilate permitted Joseph of Arimathea to house Jesus' body in his newly constructed tomb.
● The book explains what happened to Jesus during His three days in that rich man's tomb.
● On the third day, Jesus rose from the dead and appeared first to Mary Magdalene and later to dozens of followers, including eleven of His twelve Disciples.
● The Pharisees bribed the soldiers guarding the tomb to lie and say that His Disciples stole His body.
● Jesus gave His Disciples an assignment to share the good news with Jews and Gentiles worldwide.
● On the fortieth day, the Disciples witnessed Jesus ascending into Heaven.
● On Pentecost, 50 days after Jesus rose from the dead, He gave 120 followers the gift of the Holy Spirit. As a result, 3000 Jews converted.

Fifty percent (50%) of all book sales will be donated to **Covenant House** to "***join the fight to end youth homelessness***."

FYI – This is a stand-alone book pulled from 30 sections of my 75-chapter book titled, "Jesus' Crucifixion and Resurrection foretold by 12 Biblical Prophets & Kings." Those 30 sections include:

After 7 Wows, Tomb, Resurrects Bk	*Jesus' Crucifixion and Resurrection ... Book*
Chapter 1 of this book is the same as	*Chapter 40 of my other book.*
Chapter 2 of this book is the same as	*Chapter 41 of my other book.*
Chapter 3 of this book is the same as	*Chapter 42 of my other book.*
Chapter 4 of this book is the same as	*Chapter 43 of my other book.*
Chapter 5 of this book is the same as	*Chapter 44 of my other book.*
Chapter 6 of this book is the same as	*Chapter 45 of my other book.*
Chapter 7 of this book is the same as	*Chapter 46 of my other book.*
Chapter 8 of this book is the same as	*Chapter 47 of my other book.*

Chapter 9 of this book is the same as	*Chapter 48 of my other book.*
Chapter 10 of this book is the same as	*Chapter 49 of my other book.*
Study Guide for Ch. 1-10 is the same as	*Study Guide for Ch. 40-49 of my other book.*
Chapter 11 of this book is the same as	*Chapter 50 of my other book*
Chapter 12 of this book is the same as	*Chapter 51 of my other book*
Chapter 13 of this book is the same as	*Chapter 52 of my other book*
Chapter 14 of this book is the same as	*Chapter 53 of my other book*
Chapter 15 of this book is the same as	*Chapter 54 of my other book*
Chapter 16 of this book is the same as	*Chapter 55 of my other book*
Chapter 17 of this book is the same as	*Chapter 56 of my other book*
Chapter 18 of this book is the same as	*Chapter 57 of my other book*
Chapter 19 of this book is the same as	*Chapter 58 of my other book*
Chapter 20 of this book is the same as	*Chapter 59 of my other book*
Study Guide for Ch. 11-20 is same as	*Study Guide for Ch. 50-59 of my other book.*
Chapter 21 of this book is the same as	*Chapter 60 of my other book.*
Chapter 22 of this book is the same as	*Chapter 61 of my other book.*
Chapter 23 of this book is the same as	*Chapter 62 of my other book.*
Chapter 24 of this book is the same as	*Chapter 63 of my other book.*
Chapter 25 of this book is the same as	*Chapter 64 of my other book.*
Study Guide for Ch. 21-25 is same as	*Study Guide for Ch. 60-64 of my other book.*
Chapter 26 is the same as	*Chapter 74 of my other book.*
Chapter 27 is a shortened Bibliography	*found in Chapter 75 of my other book.*

Table of Contents

AFTER JESUS TOOK LAST BREATH, 7 UNANTICIPATED THINGS OCCURRED

Right after Jesus took His very last breath, 7 unanticipated things occurred.

Since Jesus was fully God plus fully man, He had the ability to die upon His own command.

1 of 7 Wows

1st of 7 WOWS after Jesus died on the Cross

Examine 4 Gospels for Clues (KJV)

Matthew 27:50	Mark 15:37	Luke 23:46	John 19:30
50 Jesus, when he had cried again with a loud voice, yielded up the ghost.	**37** And Jesus cried with a loud voice, and gave up the ghost.	**46** … and having said thus, he gave up the ghost.	**30** … He bowed his head, and gave up the ghost.

DIED ON COMMAND

John 10:17 Therefore doth my Father love me, because I lay down my life, that I might take it again. 18 No man taketh it from me, but I lay it down of myself. I have power to lay it down, and I have power to take it again. This commandment have I received of my Father. (KJV)

Let's examine what Jesus did at His death as a metaphor. Since He alone was fully God and fully man, He alone had the ability, like turning a water faucet on, to pour His Spirit into a body suit of flesh (as a baby).

Around 3 PM at that Friday crucifixion, Christ Jesus turned the water faucet off. Then, He withdrew His Spirit from His body suit of flesh.

So, on command, He, as part of the Triune God, could lay down His life and pick it up again in a soon-to-be Glorified body.

Revelation 1:1 The Revelation of Jesus Christ, which God gave unto him, to shew unto his servants things which must shortly come to pass; and he sent and signified it by his angel unto his servant John: 2 Who bare record of the word of God, and of the testimony of Jesus Christ, and of all things that he saw.

Revelation 1:5 And from Jesus Christ, who is the faithful witness, and the first begotten of the dead, and the prince of the kings of the earth. Unto him that loved us, and washed us from our sins in his own blood, 6 And hath made us kings and priests unto God and his Father; to him be glory and dominion for ever and ever. Amen.

Revelation 1:8 I am Alpha and Omega, the beginning and the ending, saith the Lord, which is, and which was, and which is to come, the Almighty.

Revelation 1:17 And when I saw him, I fell at his feet as dead. And he laid his right hand upon me, saying unto me, Fear not; I am the first and the last: 18 I am he that liveth, and was dead; and, behold, I am alive for evermore, Amen; and have the keys of hell and of death. (KJV)

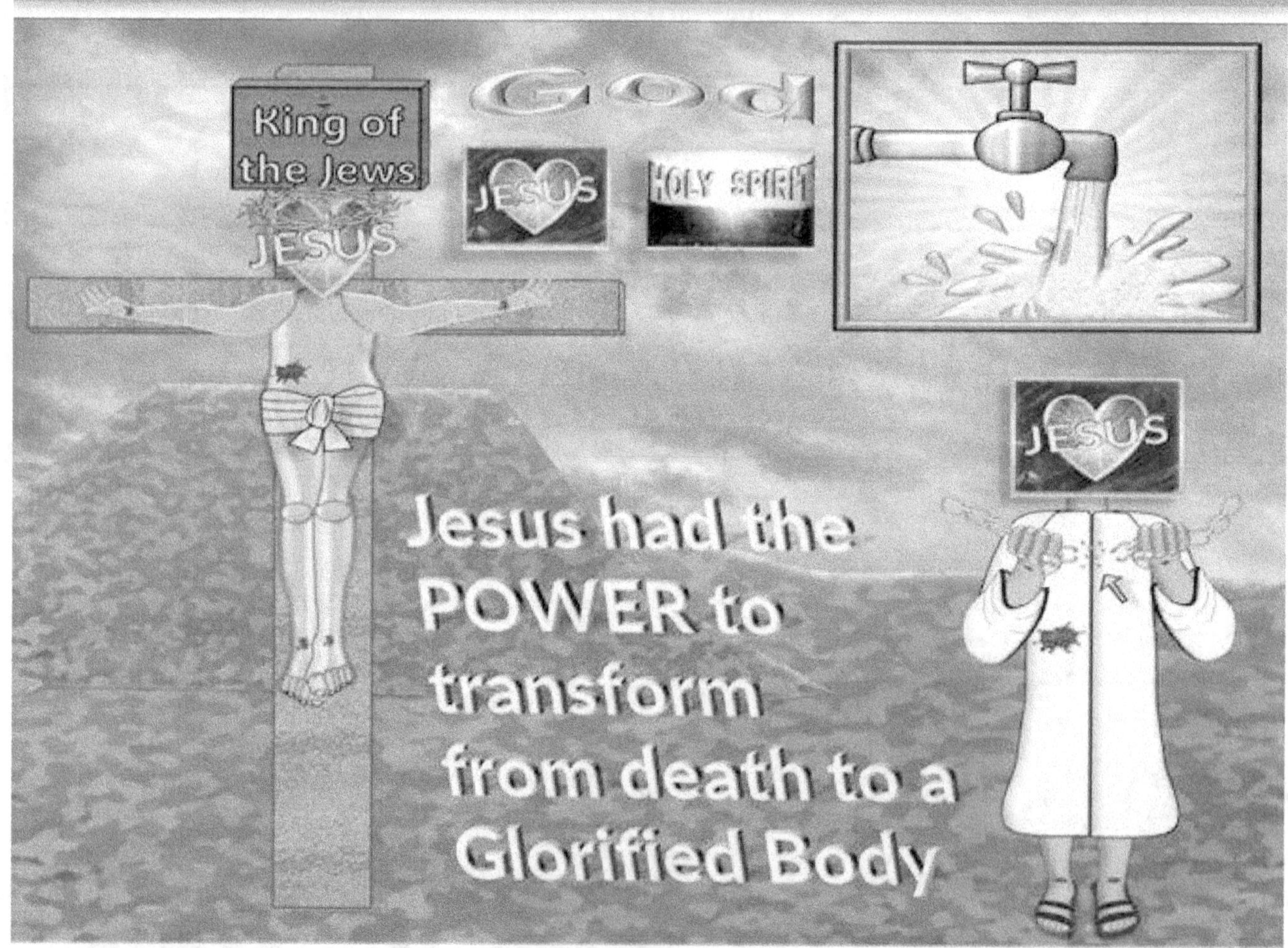

Since the Veil was Torn, Jews & Followers of Christ have open access to Holy of Holies

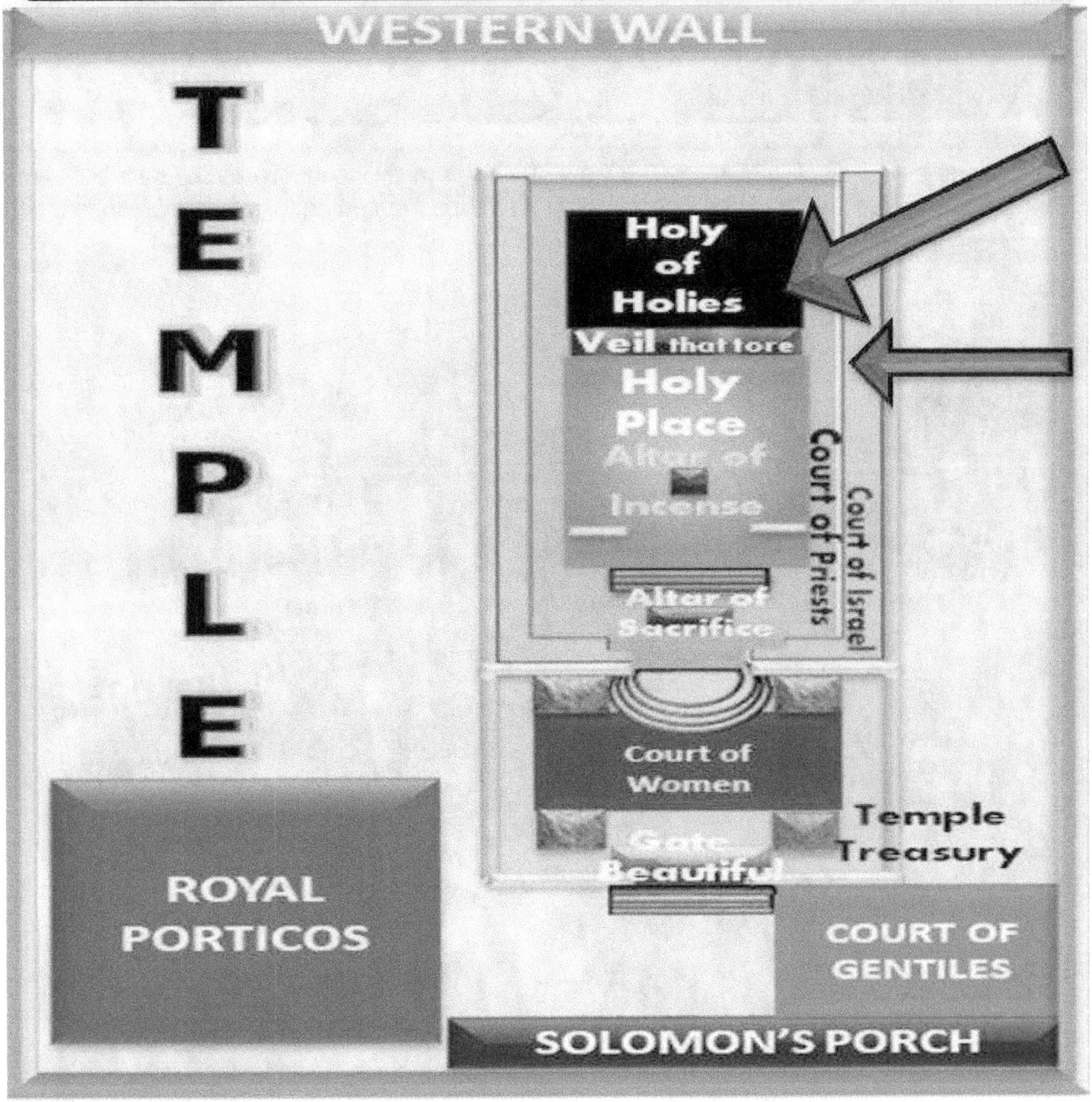

2nd of 7 WOWS after Jesus died on the Cross

Examine 4 Gospels for Clues (KJV)

Matthew 27:51	Mark 15:38	Luke 23:45	John
51 And, behold, the veil of the temple was rent in twain from the top to the bottom; and the earth did quake, and the rocks rent;	**38** And the veil of the temple was rent in twain from the top to the bottom.	**45** And the sun was darkened, and the veil of the temple was rent in the midst.	**No Reference to this Topic.**

VEIL TORN

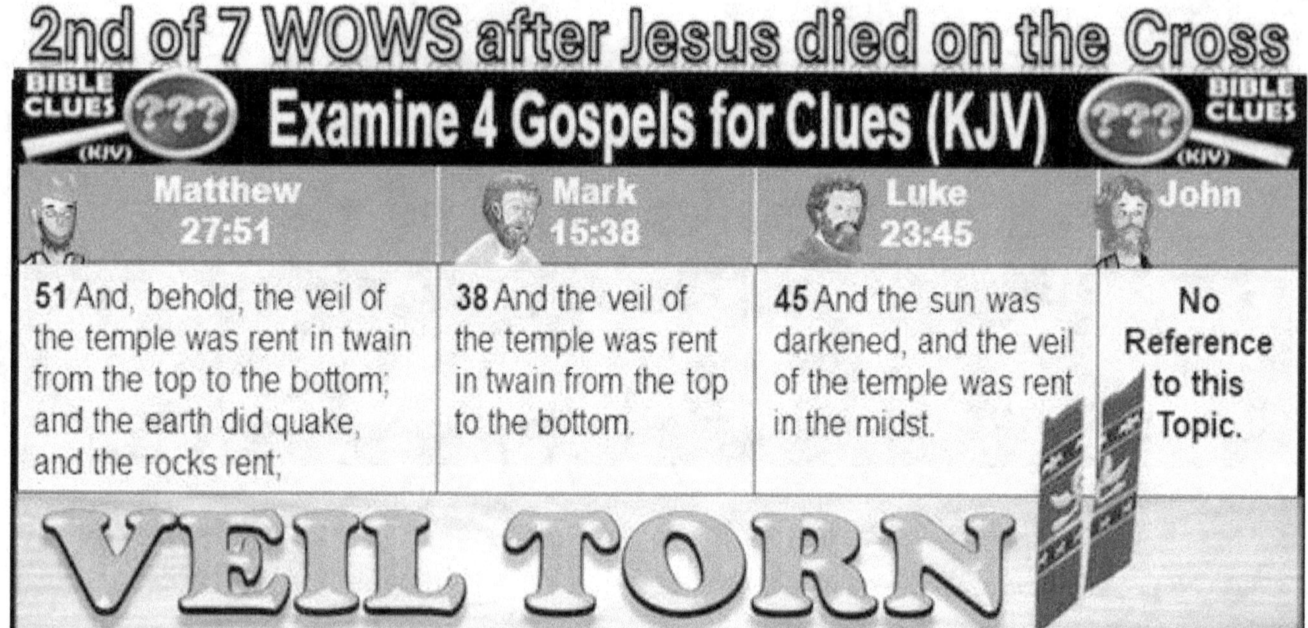

The image below displays a recreated view of what it might have looked like before 3 p.m. that Friday. Caiaphas, the High Priest, would have been attending to his various duties, not suspecting the shocking things that were about to occur.

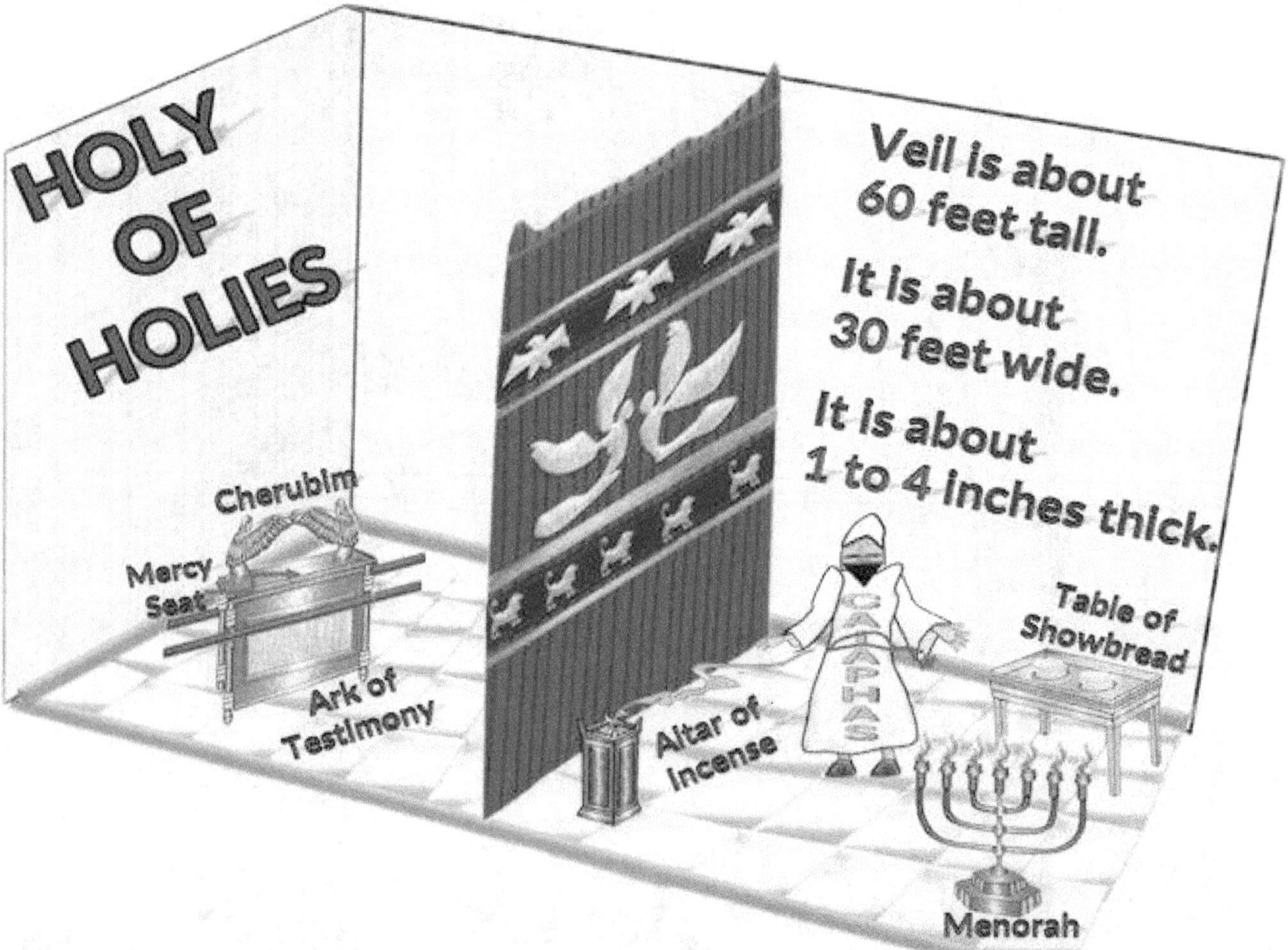

Caiaphas may have walked into the Holy Place containing the Table of Showbread, the Altar of Incense, and the Menorah. He may have stood before that 60-foot-tall Veil, recalling the previous fall when he was allowed to enter the sacred area known as the Holy of Holies. Just like with his predecessor, Aaron, the older brother of Moses, the High Priest was the only one who could enter that area. However, as stated in **Leviticus 16:2**, Aaron could only do this once a year, in the fall, on the Day of Atonement (Yom Kippur).

Caiaphas shuddered when he and the other priests read **Leviticus 10:1-2**. Tragically, two of Aaron's sons were killed by Holy Fire because they chose to disobey this Holy Ordinance.

Leviticus 10:1 Aaron's sons Nadab and Abihu took their censers, put fire in them and added incense; and they offered unauthorized fire before the Lord, contrary to his command. 2 So fire came out from the presence of the Lord and consumed them, and they died before the Lord. (NIV)

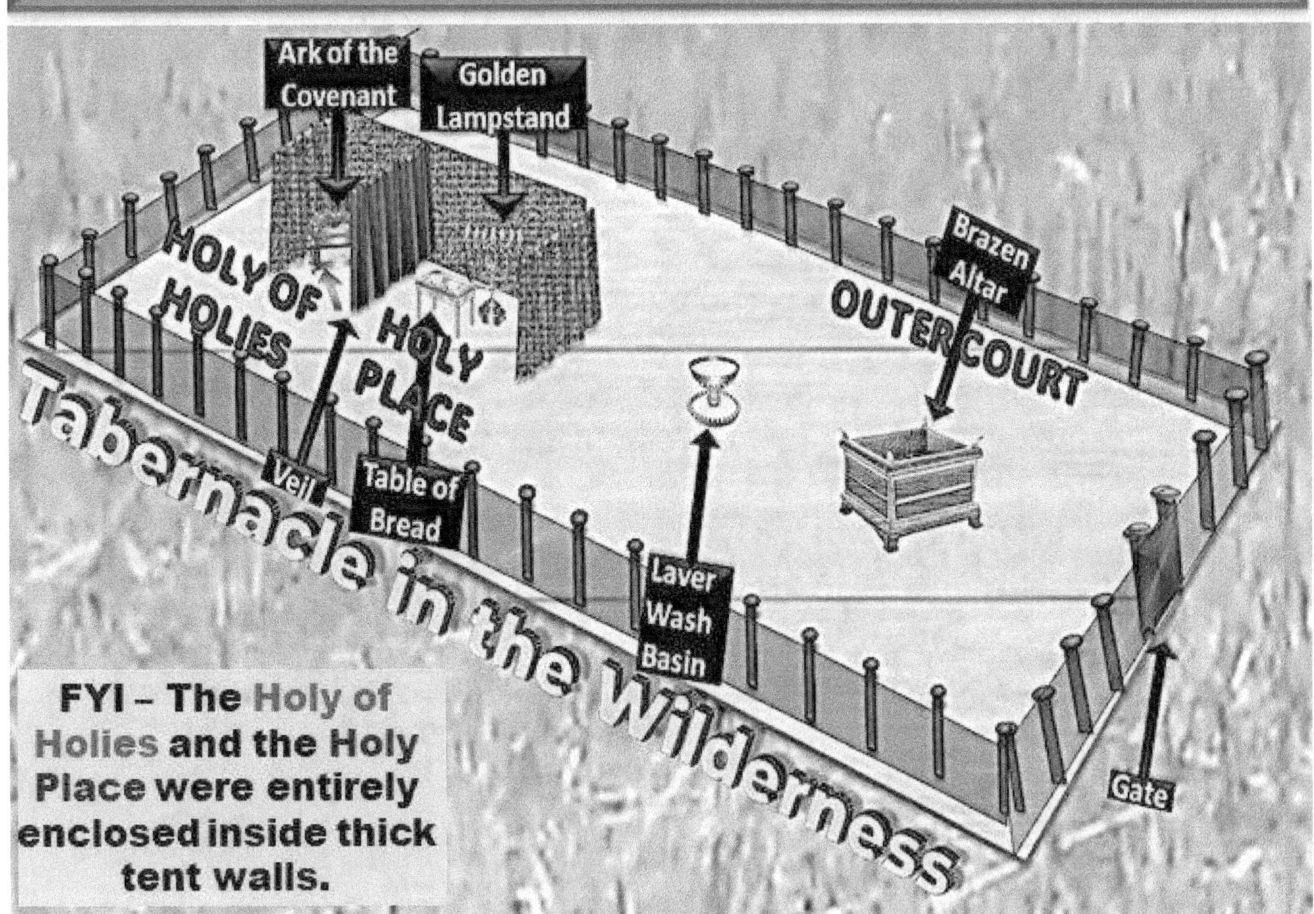

This alarming incident alerted all the priests not to take this ruling lightly.

Aaron was the first High Priest to legally enter the sacred location of the Ark of the Covenant.

During that forty-year sojourn in the wilderness, fully described in the **Book of Leviticus, Chapter 16,** High Priest Aaron would have walked through the gate along with his oldest son, Eleazar. They would have led the five animals to be sacrificed during this holy ritual.

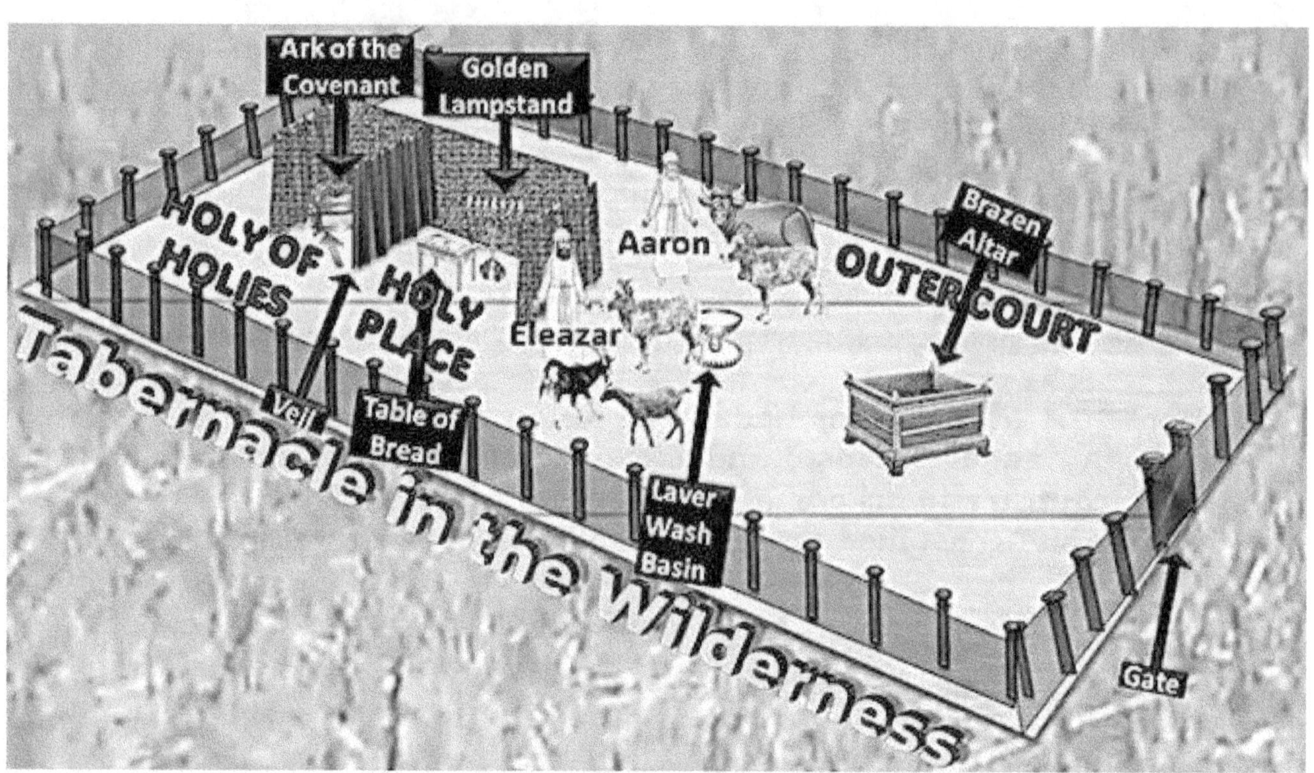

What is the purpose of the Day of Atonement or Yom Kippur in the Bible?

"The word for atonement refers broadly to reconciliation, but the word for cleansing more specifically identifies this reconciliation in terms of ritual purification. So, the Day of Atonement provided external, ceremonial purification for Israel as a nation in a special covenant relationship with God."

Bull	Ram	Ram	Goat #1	Goat #2

"The Day of Atonement ceremony was performed by the High Priest alone. Five animals were required for it: 1 bull, 2 rams, and 2 goats (Leviticus 16:1-5). The bull was a sin offering for the sins of the priest and one of the goats was a sin offering for the sins of the people."

Aaron would cleanse himself and don the holy garments of a white linen tunic and undergarments, a white linen sash or belt, and a white linen turban on his head. He would bring in a young bull from his herds representing a **SIN OFFERING** for himself, his family, and his fellow priests. He would also provide a ram for a **BURNT OFFERING**. Representing the Israelites, they would provide a ram and two male goats from their herds. **[Leviticus 16:3-6]**

In **Leviticus 16:7-10**, we learn that Aaron will cast lots to decern which of the two goats will be the **SIN OFFERING** for the Children of Israel and which one will be the **SCAPEGOAT** that shall "be presented alive before the Lord to make atonement on it; and it shall be sent into the wilderness" in that role.

GOOGLE QUOTE: "Can you eat on Day of Atonement? Yom Kippur is the Jewish Day of Atonement, and is a day (usually upward of 24 hours) for fasting, with **no food or drink."**

The Priest will tie some yarn or sash onto the horn of the goat chosen to be that year's **SCAPEGOAT.**

The High Priest will only enter the **Holy of Holies** three times. (1) The first time is when he brings in enough incense to make a cloud to cover the mercy seat on the Ark of the Covenant, as that is supposed to be where the Lord would locate Himself. Aaron would die if he did not do this and could see the Lord. **Leviticus 16:12-13** states:

Leviticus 16:12 He shall take a censer full of burning coals from the [bronze] altar before the Lord, and two handfuls of finely ground sweet incense, and bring it inside the veil [into the Most Holy Place], **13** and put the incense on the fire [in the censer] before the Lord, so that the cloud of the incense may cover the mercy seat that is on [the ark of] the Testimony, otherwise he will die. (AMP)

If you go on YouTube to watch videos about this sacred event, you will notice that the High Priest enters reverently and in a bowing fashion. Afterward, he backs out just as reverently.

(2) In preparation for the High Priest's second foray into the Holy of Holies, he will place his hand on the head of the young bull. He will picture every sin he sinned in the previous year entering the body of this innocent bull. He will also imagine the same thing happening with all the sins sinned by any member of his family or by the other priests and their families.

> **Leviticus 16:14 He shall take some of the bull's blood and sprinkle it with his finger on the east side of the mercy seat; also in front of the mercy seat he shall sprinkle some of the blood with his finger seven times. (AMP)**

We learn in **Leviticus 16:18**, High Priest Aaron "shall take some of the blood of the bull and put it on the horns of the altar on all sides." He will also do that with the blood of the goat.

Leviticus 4:7 informs us that he takes the "rest of the blood of the bull" and he shall pour this out "at the base of the altar ... which is at the doorway of the Tent of Meeting." He will also do that with the leftover blood of the goat.

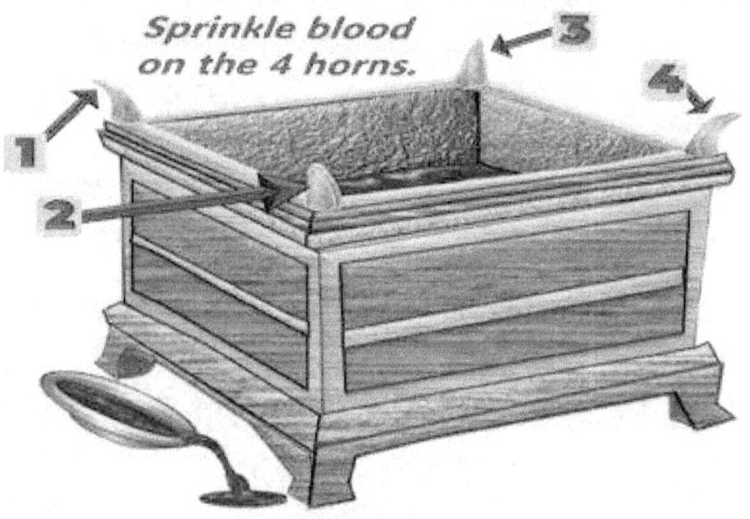

The sacrificial offering of the bull and the goat accomplishes two things. It frees the people of their sins from the previous year. It also cleanses the Holy of Holies of any built-up sin that has polluted the air, so to speak, from the transgressions of all the Children of Israel.

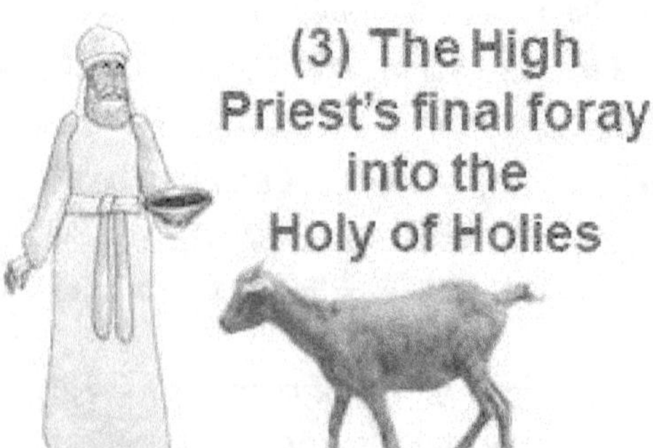

(3) The High Priest's final foray into the Holy of Holies

> **Leviticus 16:15 Then he shall kill the goat of the sin offering that is for [the sins of] the people and bring its blood within the veil [into the Most Holy Place] and do with its blood as he did with the blood of the bull, and sprinkle it on the mercy seat and in front of the mercy seat. (AMP)**

Leviticus 16:16 So he shall make atonement for the Holy Place (Holy of Holies) because of the uncleanness and transgressions of the Israelites, for all their sins. He shall also do this for the Tent of Meeting which is among them in the midst of their uncleanness (impurities). (AMP) ...

Leviticus 16:19 With his finger he shall sprinkle some of the blood on the altar of burnt offering seven times and cleanse it and consecrate it from the uncleanness of the Israelites. (AMP)

Leviticus 16:20 When he has finished atoning for the Holy Place and the Tent of Meeting and the altar, he shall present the live goat. (AMP)

Leviticus 16:21 Then Aaron shall lay both of his hands on the head of the live goat, and confess over it all the wickedness of the sons of Israel and all their transgressions in regard to all their sins; and he shall lay them on the head of the goat [the scapegoat, the sin-bearer], and send it away into the wilderness by the hand of a man who is prepared [for the task].

Leviticus 16:22 The goat shall carry on itself all their (the Israelites) wickedness, carrying them to a solitary (infertile) land; and he shall release the goat in the wilderness. (AMP)

So, just like Christ bearing our sins on the cross, this blameless SCAPEGOAT will carry all of their sins far, far away.

Some articles and videos about past celebrations of the Day of Atonement indicated that sometimes, a priest had to lead this goat as much as 10 miles away. In some cases, the goat might return. The people would cry out, "Oh, no! Our sins are coming back!" So, it became the custom to violently throw this goat over a cliff so that it would die with their sins inside of it.

Psalm 103:12 As far as the east is from the west, so far hath he removed our transgressions from us. (KJV)

Leviticus 16:23-24 describes Aaron removing the Holy Garments and leaving them there. He will wear his regular priestly garments after bathing his body with water in a holy place.

Next, he will offer the two rams as burnt offerings. One ram represents a burnt offering for himself, his family, and fellow priests. The other ram represents a burnt offering for that of all the Children of Israel. In this way, as **Leviticus 16:24** states, this will make "atonement for himself and for the people."

The man leading the SCAPEGOAT into the wilderness must wash his clothes and bathe before returning to the camp.

Leviticus 16:25 And he shall offer up in smoke the fat of the sin offering on the altar. ...

Leviticus 16:27 The bull for the sin offering and the goat for the sin offering, whose blood was brought in to make atonement in the Holy Place (Holy of Holies), shall be taken outside the camp; their skins, their meat, and their waste shall be burned in the fire. (AMP)

Leviticus 16:29-34 states the following directives:

 The Day of Atonement will happen annually on the tenth day of the seventh month.

1st month of year of the Jewish calendar -   Nisan (March – April)
2nd month of year of the Jewish calendar –   Iyyar (April – May)
3rd month of year of the Jewish calendar –   Sivan (May – June)
4th month of year of the Jewish calendar –   Tammuz (June – July)
5th month of year of the Jewish calendar –   Av (July – August)
6th month of year of the Jewish calendar –   Elul (August – September)
7th month of year of the Jewish calendar –   Tishrei (September – October)
8th month of year of the Jewish calendar –   Heshvan (October – November)
9th month of year of the Jewish calendar –   Kislev (November – December)
10th month of year of the Jewish calendar –   Tevet (December – January)
11th month of year of the Jewish calendar –   Shevat (January – February)
12th month of year of the Jewish calendar –   Adar (February – March)

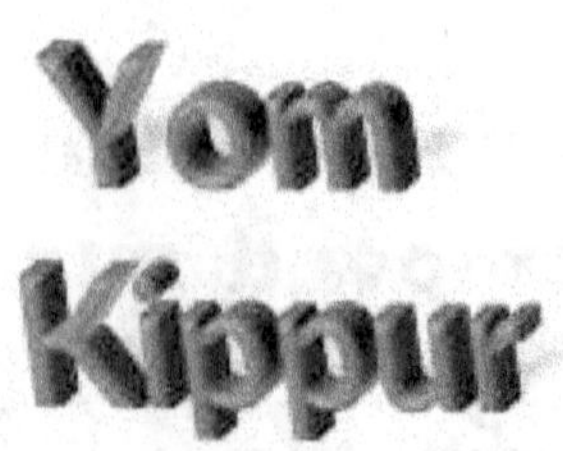

FYI – In 30 AD, Yom Kippur occurred on Tishrei (or Tishri 10, 3791) which would have been September 25th of the year 30 AD.

Another example: In 2024, Yom Kippur will begin at sunset on Friday, October 11, 2024 and end at sunset on Saturday, October 12, 2024.

2 **Leviticus 16:29** directs that the people will "humble yourselves [by fasting] and not do any work.

3 **Leviticus 16:30** "for it is on this day that atonement shall be made for you, to cleanse you; you will be clean from all your sins before the Lord."

4 **Leviticus 16:31** indicates that this is a permanent statute. "It is a Sabbath of solemn rest for you."

5 **Leviticus 16:32-33** describe how the priest who conducts this ceremony is anointed and ordained to do so. He shall wear the holy garments so he can make atonement for the Holy Sanctuary, the altar, the priests, and the people.

6 **Leviticus 16:34** "This shall be a permanent statute for you, so that atonement may be made for the children of Israel for all their sins once a year."

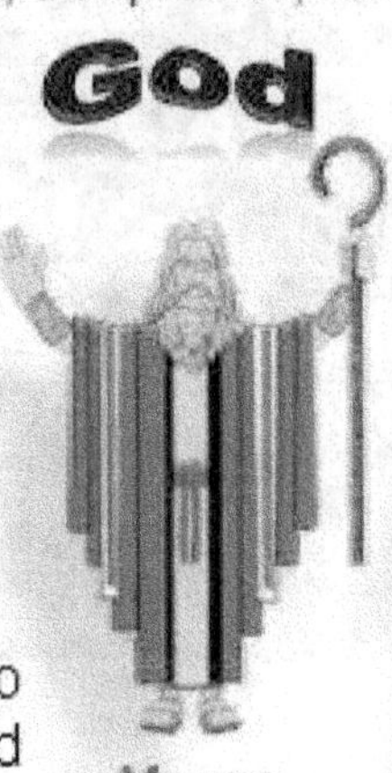

7 So God told this to Moses. Moses then told this to Aaron.

So, let's return to Caiaphas in the Jerusalem Temple. Presuming that Jesus was crucified in 30 AD, Caiaphas would be looking ahead to **Tishri 10, 3791 which would have been September 25th of the year 30 AD.**

He might have been looking back to the first time he conducted this ceremony in 18 AD. He likely felt quite nervous and awed to enter the **Holy of Holies** area that very first time. Since that day, he probably felt more pride than fear since he had already served in that role for 11 years.

Did Caiaphas feel like he would need to atone for orchestrating Jesus' death? Or would he find some way to rationalize it to his satisfaction? Was there any part of Caiaphas feeling a case of nerves that it had been dark as night from 12 noon that very day? Did he even guess that it might have been a form of God's judgment against him?

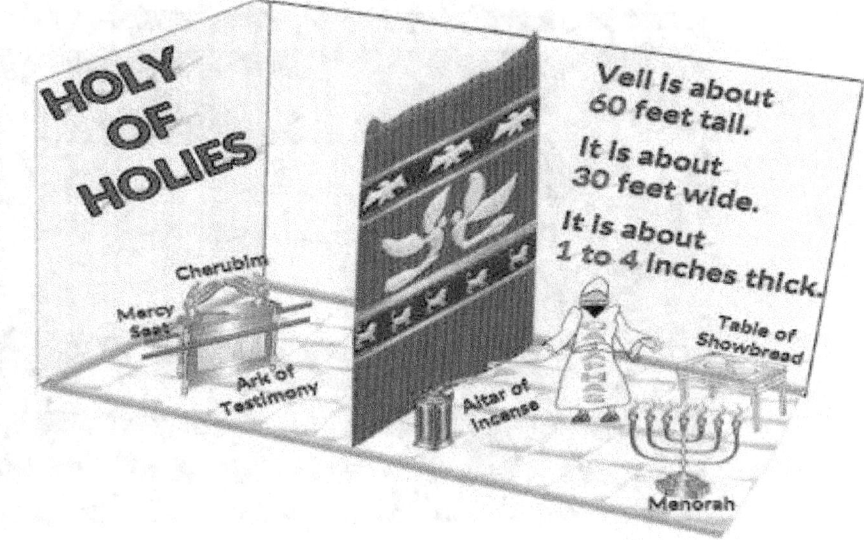

"What day was Passover when Jesus died? John indicates that Jesus died as the paschal lambs were being slaughtered for a "high day"--a double holy day when Passover and the Sabbath coincided (see John 13:1; 18:28; 18;39; 19:14; 19:31). Calender experts tell us that this date was most likely April 7, A.D. 30."

"What time was the Passover eaten? Note that though the sacrifice of the Passover lamb occurred on the afternoon Nisan 14, the ceremonial eating of the meal, or the "seder," would begin later, just before sundown and continue throughout the night."

This is what Caiaphas got to visit once each year on the Day of Atonement.
A close-up look at a replica of the Ark of the Covenant and its sacred contents:

"The Ark of the Covenant, also known as the Ark of the Testimony or the Ark of God, is believed to have been the most sacred religious relic of the Israelites. It is described as a wooden chest coated in pure gold and topped off by an elaborate golden lid known as the mercy seat."

How heavy was the veil in the Jerusalem temple?

"The veil of the temple was woven from blue, purple, crimson and white thread, and embroidered with cherubim (2 Chron.3.14); the veil in the tabernacle had been similar, (Exod.26.31; 36.35), It was a valuable piece of fabric, and both Antiochus and Titus took a veil when they looted the temple (1 Mac.1.21-2; Josephus War 7.162). In the second temple it was some two hundred square metres of fabric and when it contracted uncleanness and had to be washed, three hundred priests were needed for the job (m.Shekalim 8.4-5). Josephus says it was a Babylonian tapestry (War 5.212), a curtain embroidered with a panorama of the heavens (War 5.213). The veil separated the holy place from the most holy (Exod.26.33), screening from view the ark and the cherubim or, in the temple, the ark and the chariot throne. We are told that only the high priest entered the holy of holies, once a year on the Day of Atonement."

I surmise that Caiaphas felt great pride and hubris over his preferential position in the Temple.

Proverbs 16:18 Pride goeth before destruction, and an haughty spirit before a fall.

Proverbs 16:19 Better it is to be of an humble spirit with the lowly, than to divide the spoil with the proud.

Proverbs 16:20 He that handleth a matter wisely shall find good: and whoso trusteth in the Lord, happy is he. (KJV)

Did Caiaphas' conscience prick him over the commandments he broke that day?

The 10 Commandments

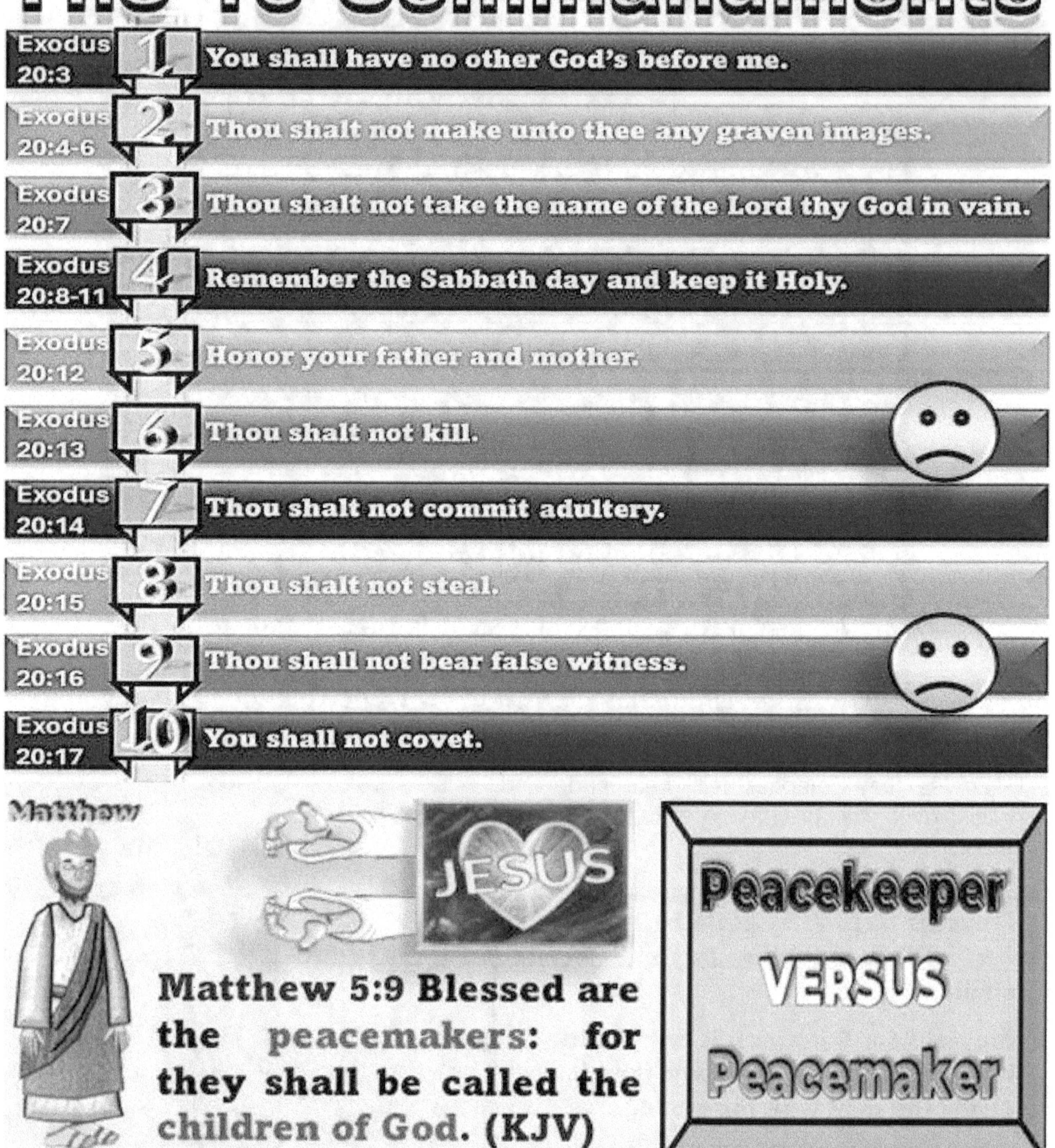

In the winter/spring 2024, my church studied the Beatitudes Jesus preached on the Sermon on the Mount. It struck me as very interesting to notice that the very day I planned to complete this section about the veil was the day the pastor focused his sermon on **Matthew 5:9**. I couldn't help pondering how this applied to Caiaphas and the Roman soldiers as the pastor described PEACEMAKERS (Christ-centered) versus PEACEKEEPERS (satisfying self)

Consider the Roman officers and soldiers. They maintained a PEACEKEEPING role in the empire. Their mantra might have been, **"Act with decorum and follow our rules, or we will knock a few heads together, kill you, or throw you in prison."**

The Sanhedrin wanted to maintain peace so they could preserve their power base. Additionally, they desired this to avoid the Jewish people provoking the Roman soldiers. Imagine their state of mind when Jesus came along preaching peace, agape Love, and following God's actual laws as opposed to their idea of God's rules, laws, commandments, and precepts. Eventually, Caiaphas and the priests came to the following PEACEKEEPING conclusion:

> **John 11:47 Then gathered the chief priests and the Pharisees a council, and said, What do we? for this man doeth many miracles. 48 If we let him thus alone, all men will believe on him: and the Romans shall come and take away both our place and nation.**
>
> **John 11:49 And one of them, named Caiaphas, being the high priest that same year, said unto them, Ye know nothing at all, 50 Nor consider that it is expedient for us, that one man should die for the people, and that the whole nation perish not.**
>
> **John 11:51 And this spake he not of himself: but being high priest that year, he prophesied that Jesus should die for that nation; 52 And not for that nation only, but that also he should gather together in one the children of God that were scattered abroad. 53 Then from that day forth they took counsel together for to put him to death.**

The time was creeping closer and closer to 3 PM – the moment of Jesus' death. I imagine God orchestrated it so that Caiaphas stood in front of the Veil so that he could witness and perhaps comprehend the enormity of the crime he and his subordinates had committed.

In **Matthew 27:51**, Matthew pointed out that the Veil tore before the earthquake so that Caiaphas couldn't blame an earthquake for tearing it. Additionally, Matthew states, "**the veil of the temple was rent in twain from the top to the bottom**." Remember the veil was 60-feet tall and 1 to 4 inches thick.

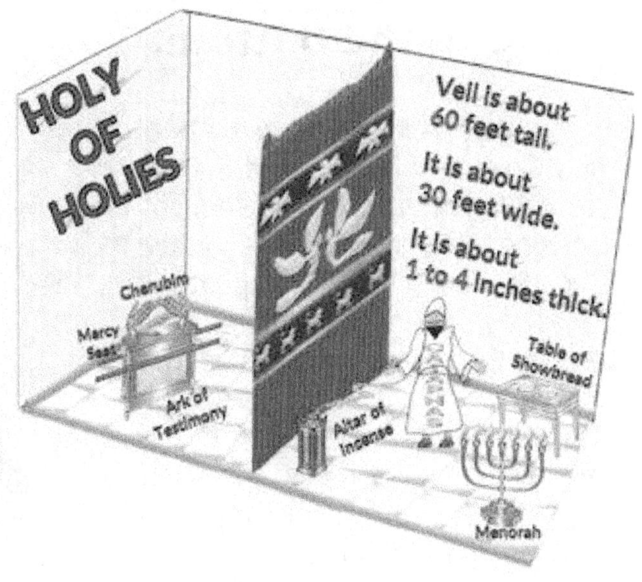

Hebrews 9:2 A tabernacle was set up. In its first room were the lampstand and the table with its consecrated bread; this was called the Holy Place.

Hebrews 9:3 Behind the second curtain was a room called the Most Holy Place, 4 which had the golden altar of incense and the gold-covered ark of the covenant. This ark contained the gold jar of manna, Aaron's staff that had budded, and the stone tablets of the covenant.

Hebrews 9:5 Above the ark were the cherubim of the Glory, overshadowing the atonement cover.

Hebrews 9:6 When everything had been arranged like this, the priests entered regularly into the outer room to carry on their ministry. 7 But only the high priest entered the inner room, and that only once a year, and never without blood, which he offered for himself and for the sins the people had committed in ignorance. (NIV)

At the moment when Jesus died, the Veil tore from the top to the bottom.

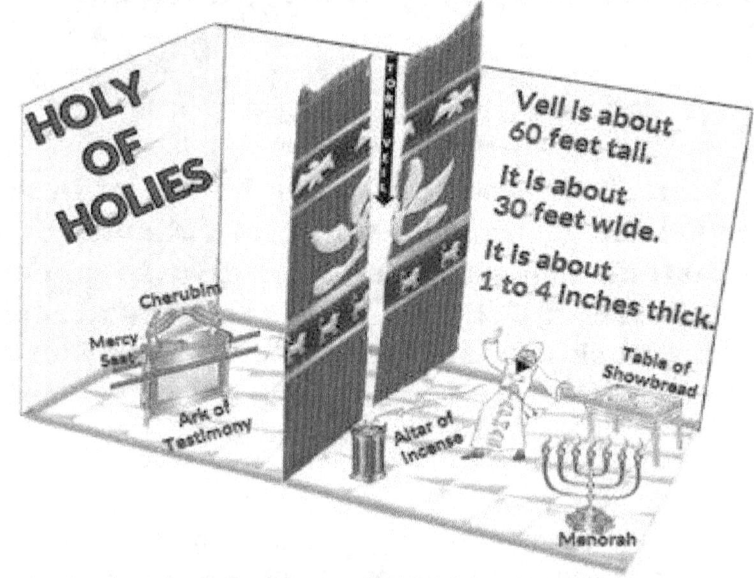

From that day forward, the Ark of the Covenant (also called the Ark of Testimony) could be seen by anyone visiting that part of the temple. Therefore, Caiaphas or anyone could no longer attempt to box-in God. Because Jesus chose to die on the Cross for our sakes, be resurrected, ascend to His Father, and send us the Holy Spirit, everyone worldwide has open access to God 24/7.

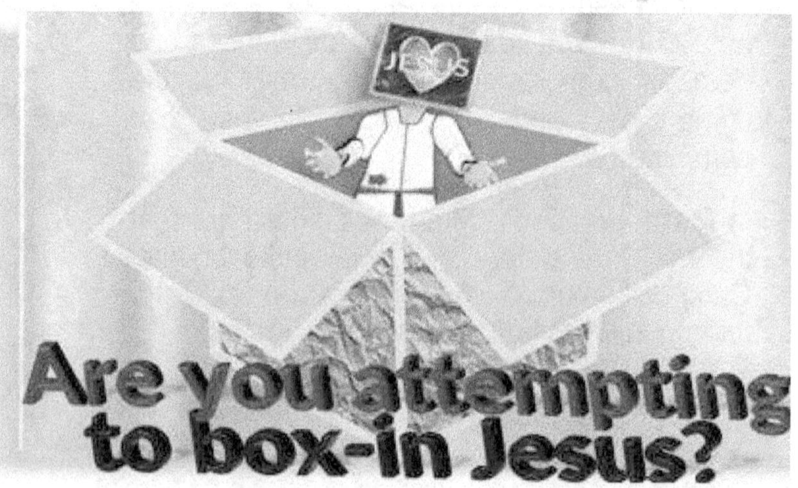

There was an Earthquake after Jesus took His last breath.

Disciple Matthew reported this strange occurrence after Jesus died.

Matthew 27:52 The earth shook, the rocks split ... (NIV)

The Bible does not reveal any further details about this. In my imagination, I picture God, the Holy Spirit, and the Heavenly Angels in tears over what Jesus had to suffer to save us. Thank you, Jesus!

There was not a tornado, but part of me found it satisfying to imagine at least one of the mocking, jeering Pharisees having a brief nightmare about a tornado sucking him into a mini lake of fire. Of course, he would awaken to find himself safe in bed. I just wanted him to regret what he had done.

Christians must be vigilant about forgiving others, whether the transgression was toward them, people they care about, or even people we read about in the Bible or past or current news. Why is that important? Even though the Holy Spirit can protect us from demons possessing us, He cannot prevent us from opening a door (or window) to a demon oppressing us if we choose to be bitter, vengeful, or unforgiving. Allowing in those negative spirits and principalities gives Satan a legal foothold on our Souls.

Ephesians 4:26 is a Remez for **Psalm 4:4** "Tremble and do not sin; when you are on your beds, search your hearts and be silent." (NIV)

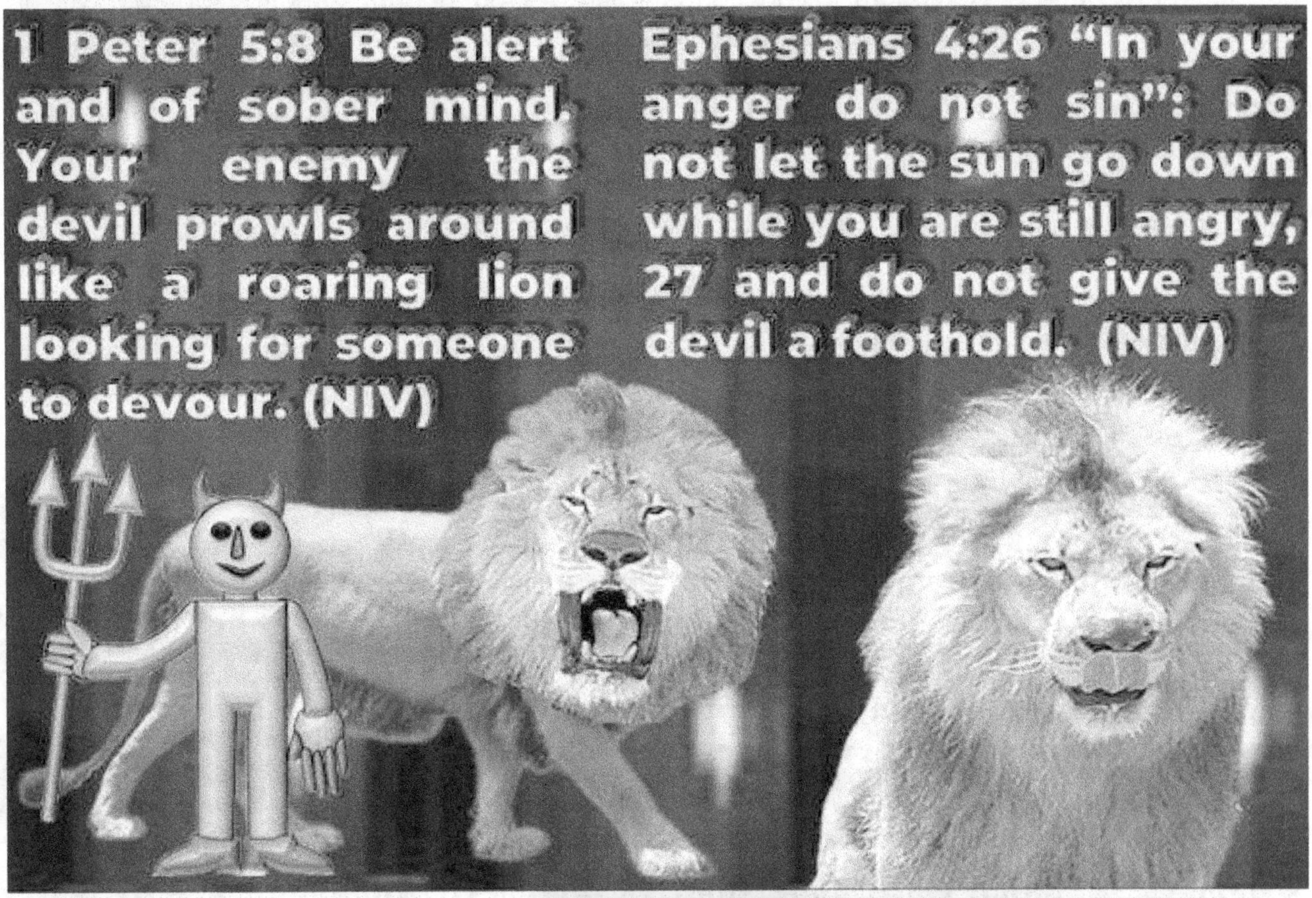

So, what action step should we take to get back in the good graces of the Triune God: our Heavenly Father, the Holy Spirit, and our Redeemer, Jesus? Like Markham's 'Outwitted' poem, we must encircle that person in forgiveness, no matter what. We're not required to forget, but God commands us to forgive.

From "Outwitted" poem by Edwin Markham

"He drew a circle to shut me out.
Heretic, rebel, a thing to flout.
But love and I had the wit to win:
We drew a circle that took him in."

We might say words like the following:

I forgive you!

• Just like Jesus forgave me my transgressions, I forgive you. After all, it is not my place to judge or convict you. That is between you and God. May God bless you and teach you what He would like you to do from now on.

• Heavenly Father, Holy Spirit, King Jesus, I know you do not sanction or approve of antisemitic words, attitudes, or behaviors. We should agape love our Jewish brothers and sisters just as we agape love all people on this planet. That does not mean we have to approve of what some individuals do. For example, we do not have to approve of the ways the Pharisees plotted to have Jesus killed. But we still need to agape love them and not judge them. After all, Jesus died on the cross just as much for them as He did for the rest of us. Consider this also. It is because Jesus died as the perfect sacrificial lamb, who had never sinned, that we are forever redeemed and have the chance not to have our sins count against us. So, perhaps, they played a role God assigned to them in advance to help make that happen. The same goes for Judas Iscariot. Maybe he also volunteered in advance to play the role he did. We will never know until we get our questions answered when the day comes that we take our last breath here and our first breath in Heaven. Think on these verses:

Ephesians 4:29 Do not let any unwholesome talk come out of your mouths, but only what is helpful for building others up according to their needs, that it may benefit those who listen. 30 And do not grieve the Holy Spirit of God, with whom you were sealed for the day of redemption. 31 Get rid of all bitterness, rage and anger, brawling and slander, along with every form of malice. 32 Be kind and compassionate to one another, forgiving each other, just as in Christ God forgave you. (NIV)

James 4:7 Submit yourselves, then, to God. Resist the devil, and he will flee from you. (NIV)

2 Corinthians 5:17 Therefore, if anyone is in Christ, the new creation has come: The old has gone, the new is here! 18 All this is from God, who reconciled us to himself through Christ and gave us the ministry of reconciliation: 19 that God was reconciling the world to himself in Christ, not counting people's sins against them. And he has committed to us the message of reconciliation. 20 We are therefore Christ's ambassadors, as though God were making his appeal through us. We implore you on Christ's behalf: Be reconciled to God. 21 God made him who had no sin to be sin for us, so that in him we might become the righteousness of God. (NIV)

Some Tombs of Holy People opened, and they were seen walking.

4 of 7 Wows

Disciple Matthew reported this strange occurrence after Jesus died.

> Matthew 27:52 ... and the tombs broke open. The bodies of many holy people who had died were raised to life. 53 They came out of the tombs after Jesus' resurrection and went into the holy city and appeared to many people. (NIV)

? How many nights and days were they alive for?

? Did they visit family, friends, or their former homes?

? Were witnesses terrified, encouraged, or in shock?

? Did they have clothes on or tomb wrappings?

? Were they taken to Heaven after this visitation?

? Did they have to return to their tombs or stay alive?

? How many holy people revived? Who were they?

? How did they react after viewing three crosses and

? hear that Jesus had returned to life?

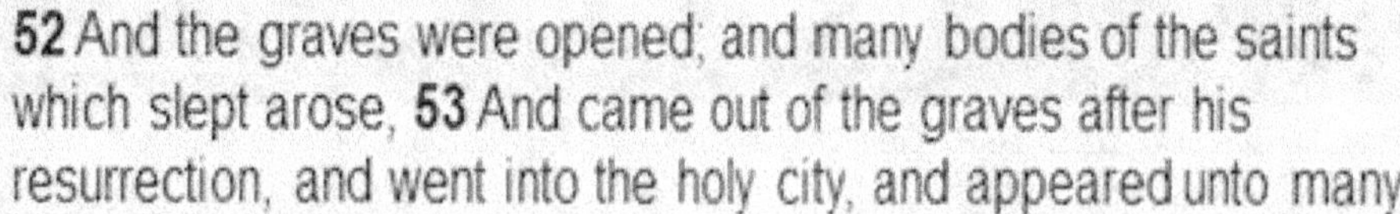

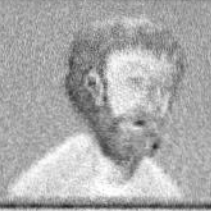

Matthew 27:52-53	Mark, Luke, & John
52 And the graves were opened; and many bodies of the saints which slept arose, **53** And came out of the graves after his resurrection, and went into the holy city, and appeared unto many.	**No Reference to this Topic.**

REMEZ – Hidden Messages

Ezekiel 37:12 Therefore prophesy and say unto them, Thus saith the Lord God; Behold, O my people, I will open your graves, and cause you to come up out of your graves, and bring you into the land of Israel. **(KJV)**

Based on Matthew's wording of **Matthew 27:52-53** and conjecture, this is what I imagined happened. It was dark in the middle of the afternoon. The veil was torn from top to bottom, so human hands could not have done it. Next, there was an earthquake. During or right after this earthquake, several graves opened up.

Just like Lazarus [**John 11:1-44**] and Jairus' daughter [**Matthew 9:18–19, 23-26**; **Mark 5:21–24, 35-43**; and **Luke 8:40-42, 49–56**], they may have lay their blinking and trying to make sense of things. Perhaps they peeked out and saw Jesus hanging on the cross. They might have supernaturally known who Jesus was in those moments and lay back down pondering what they saw. They did not yet have the strength to walk for the rest of that Friday and all during the Sabbath (i.e., Saturday). Then, after Jesus, the 'first fruit,' resurrected, strength poured into their limbs on Sunday. They left their graves, entered the Holy City, and appeared to former family members, friends, and acquaintances.

We will never know whether they spent just one day, a few days, or a few years with these people or went to Paradise along with the thief who died on the right-hand cross to Christ. The Bible does not say. What do you think happened with them?

1 Corinthians 15:20 But now [as things really are] Christ has in fact been raised from the dead, [and He became] the first fruits [that is, the first to be resurrected with an incorruptible, immortal body, foreshadowing the resurrection] of those who have fallen asleep [in death]. 21 For since [it was] by a man that death came [into the world], it is also by a Man that the resurrection of the dead has come. 22 For just as in Adam all die, so also in Christ all will be made alive. (AMP)

Tomb on
Friday & Saturday

Tomb on
EASTER
morning

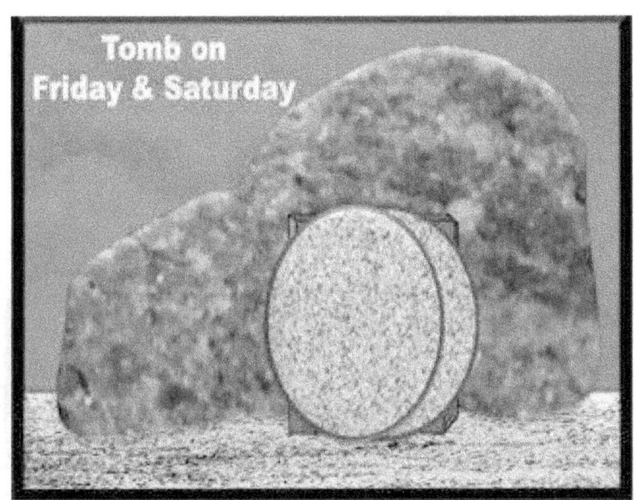

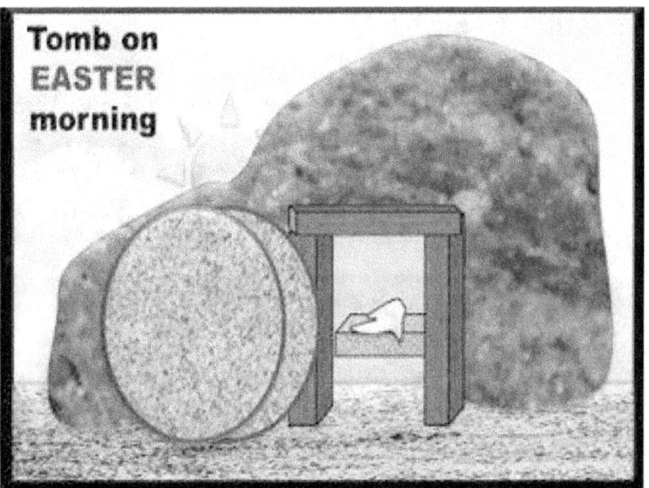

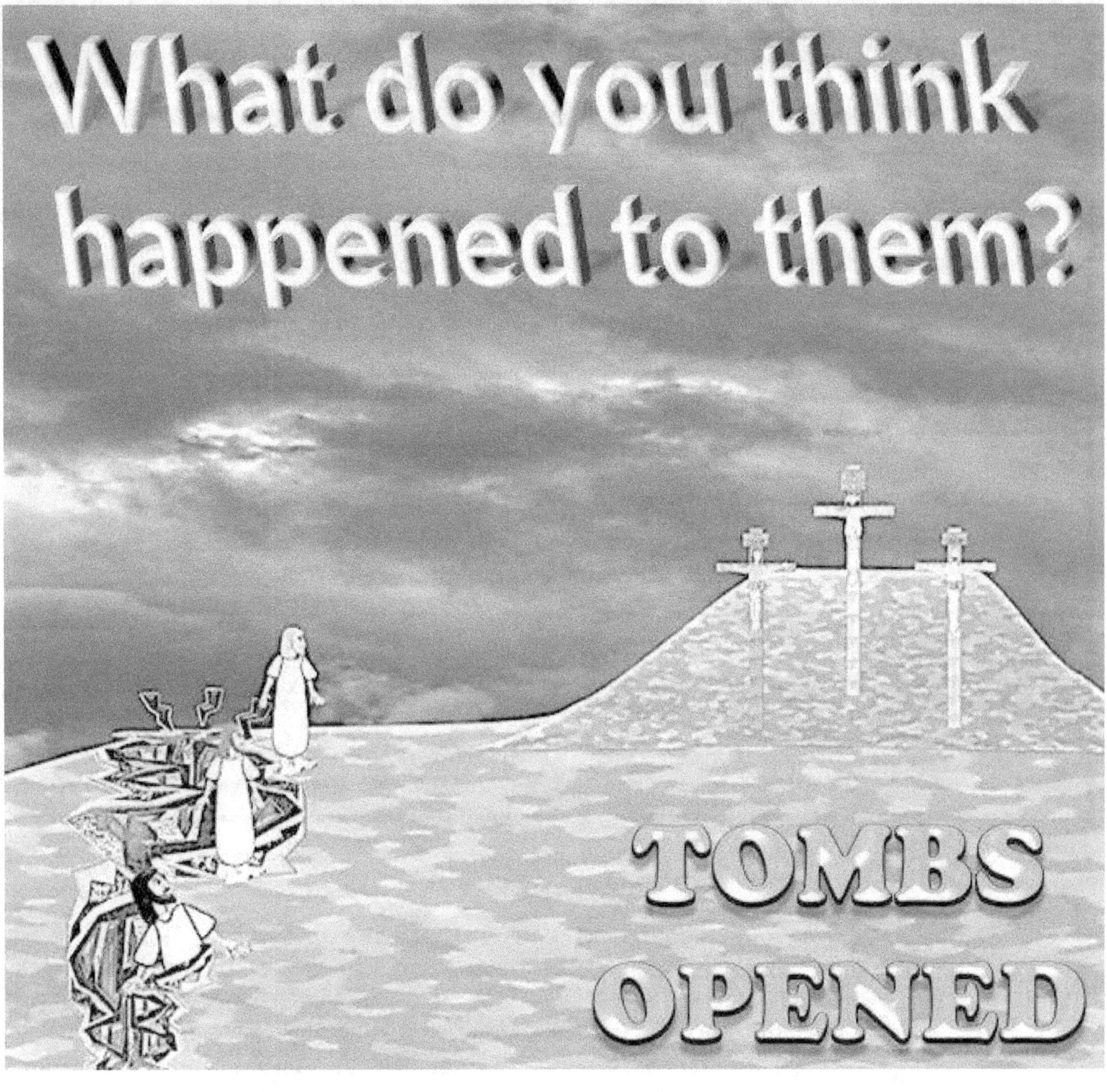
What do you think happened to them?
TOMBS
OPENED

Roman Centurion viewed all this and concluded that Jesus must truly be the Son of God.

5 of 7 Wows

5th of 7 WOWS after Jesus died on the Cross

Examine 4 Gospels for Clues (KJV)

Matthew 27:54	Mark 15:39	Luke 23:47	John
54 Now when the centurion, and they that were with him, watching Jesus, saw the earthquake, and those things that were done, they feared greatly, saying, **Truly this was the Son of God.**	**39** And when the centurion, which stood over against him, saw that he so cried out, and gave up the ghost, he said, **Truly this man was the Son of God.**	**47** Now when the centurion saw what was done, he glorified God, saying, **Certainly this was a righteous man.**	**No Reference to this Topic.**

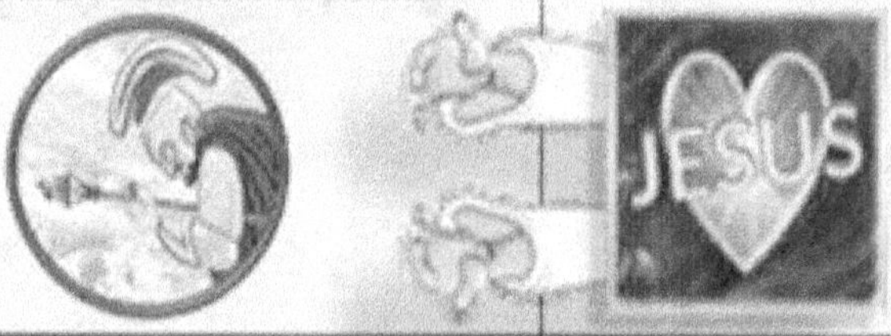

SOLDIER SAID ...

Could it have been the Roman soldier who speared Jesus on His side who came to this conclusion?

I highly recommend reading '**The Robe**' by Lloyd C. Douglas. In his Biblical reimagined tale, the Roman tribune ordered to crucify Jesus, gambled for and won Jesus' robe. In this page-turning book, you learn how he became a staunch Christian, leading many people to Christ. On Amazon, his Kindle eBook costs only $1.99.

After viewing Jesus' mangled body, some people beat their chests in true despair as they left the site.

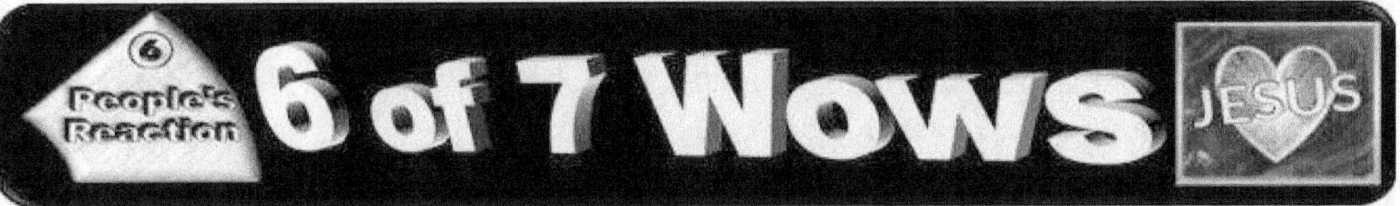

The physician named Luke, a future companion for Paul of Tarsus, was the only one who reported the following detail about how people reacted to seeing Jesus' dead and mangled body upon the cross.

> **Luke 23:48 When all the people who had gathered to witness this sight saw what took place, they beat their breasts and went away. (NIV)**

Admittedly, given that I have often been in tears while researching and writing about the pain Jesus had to endure to save us, it relieves me to hear that there were compassionate people who were also loyal to our Lord.

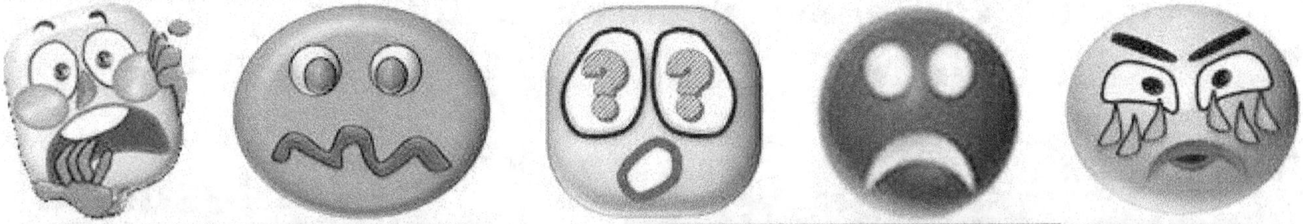

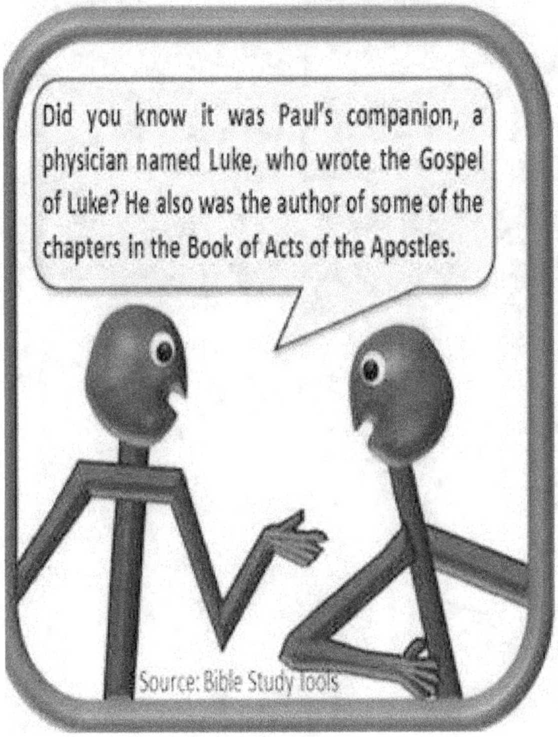

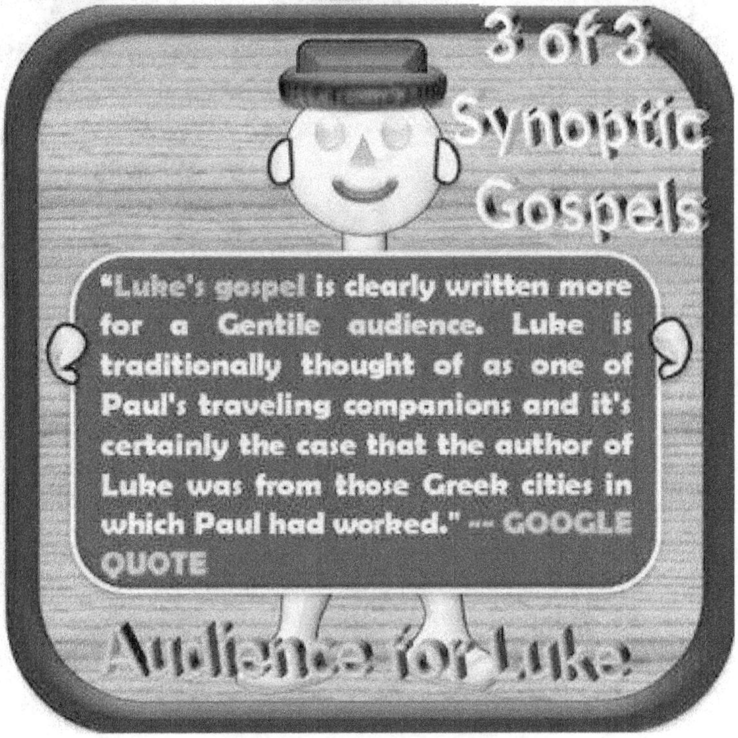

BIBLE CLUES (KJV) ??? Examine 4 Gospels for Clues (KJV) ??? BIBLE CLUES (KJV)

Luke 23:48	Matthew, Mark, & John
48 And all the people that came together to that sight, beholding the things which were done, smote their breasts, and returned.	No Reference to this Topic.

PEOPLE'S REACTION

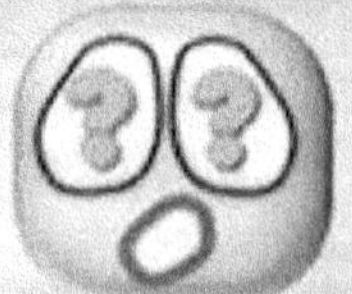

GOOGLE QUOTE: "What does smote their breasts mean in the Bible? The NLT renders this as going "home in deep sorrow" with a footnote adding, "literally, went home beating their breasts. Beating the breast was a sign of sorrow and mourning." The NIV footnote adds, "beat their breasts". A sign of anguish, grief, or contrition."

BIBLE CLUES ??? (KJV) — Examine 4 Gospels for Clues (KJV) — ??? BIBLE CLUES (KJV)

Matthew 27:55-56	Mark 15:40-41	Luke 23:49	John 19:25-27
55 And many women were there beholding afar off, which followed Jesus from Galilee, ministering unto him: **56** Among which was Mary Magdalene, and Mary the mother of James and Joses, and the mother of Zebedees children.	**40** There were also women looking on afar off: among whom was Mary Magdalene, and Mary the mother of James the less and of Joses, and Salome; **41** (Who also, when he was in Galilee, followed him, and ministered unto him;) and many other women which came up with him unto Jerusalem.	**49** And all his acquaintance, and the women that followed him from Galilee, stood afar off, beholding these things.	**25** Now there stood by the cross of Jesus his mother, and his mother's sister, Mary the wife of Cleophas, and Mary Magdalene. **26** When Jesus therefore saw his mother, and the disciple standing by, whom he loved, he saith unto his mother, **Woman, behold thy son!** **27** Then saith he to the disciple, **Behold thy mother!** And from that hour that disciple took her unto his own home.

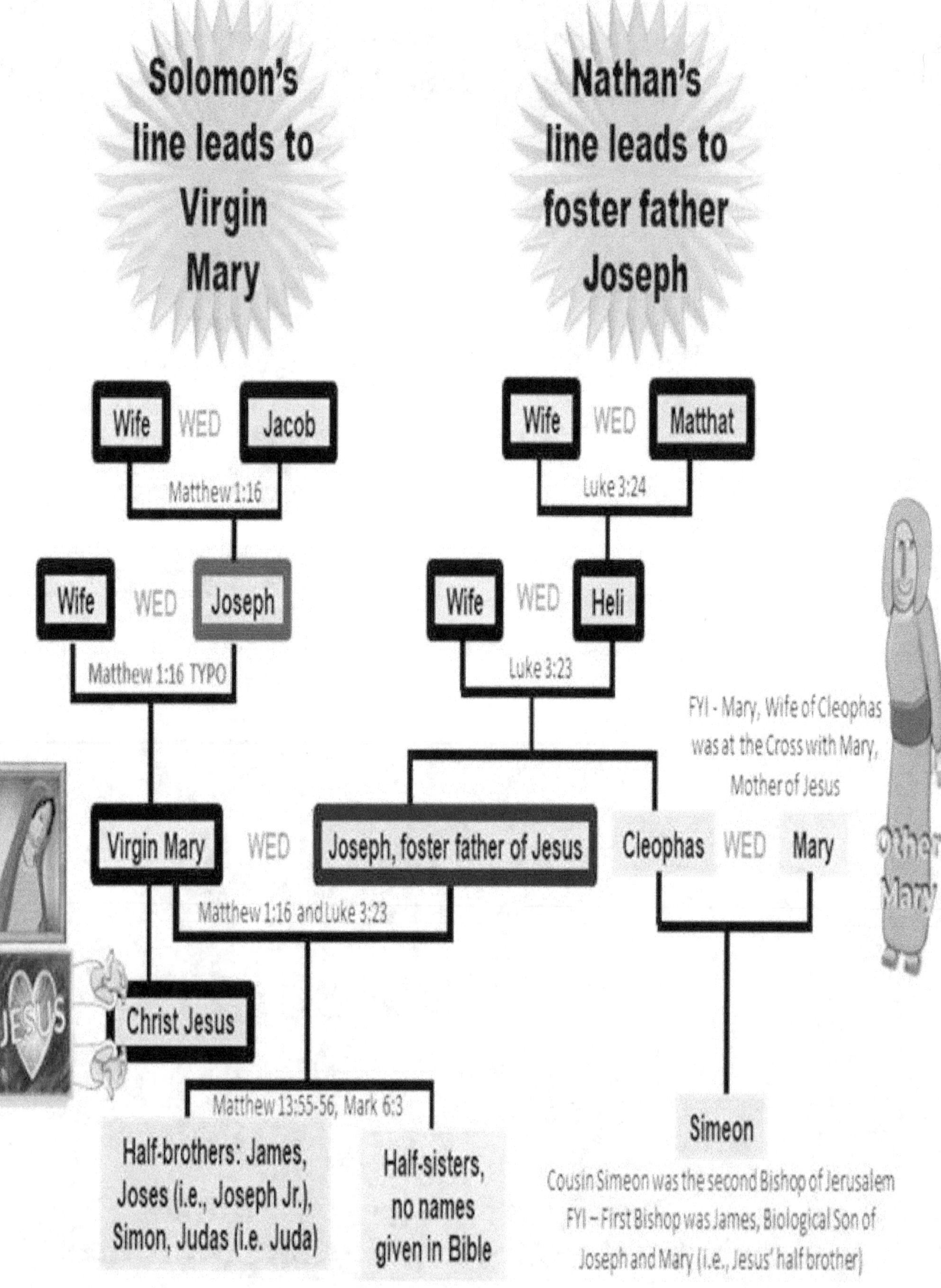

Solomon's line leads to Virgin Mary
Nathan's line leads to foster father Joseph
Wife   WED   Jacob
Matthew 1:16
Wife   WED   Matthat
Luke 3:24
Wife   WED   Joseph
Matthew 1:16 TYPO
Wife   WED   Heli
Luke 3:23
Virgin Mary   WED   Joseph, foster father of Jesus
Matthew 1:16 and Luke 3:23
Cleophas   WED   Mary
FYI - Mary, Wife of Cleophas was at the Cross with Mary, Mother of Jesus
Other Mary
Christ Jesus
JESUS
Matthew 13:55-56, Mark 6:3
Half-brothers: James, Joses (i.e., Joseph Jr.), Simon, Judas (i.e. Juda)
Half-sisters, no names given in Bible
Simeon
Cousin Simeon was the second Bishop of Jerusalem
FYI – First Bishop was James, Biological Son of Joseph and Mary (i.e., Jesus' half brother)

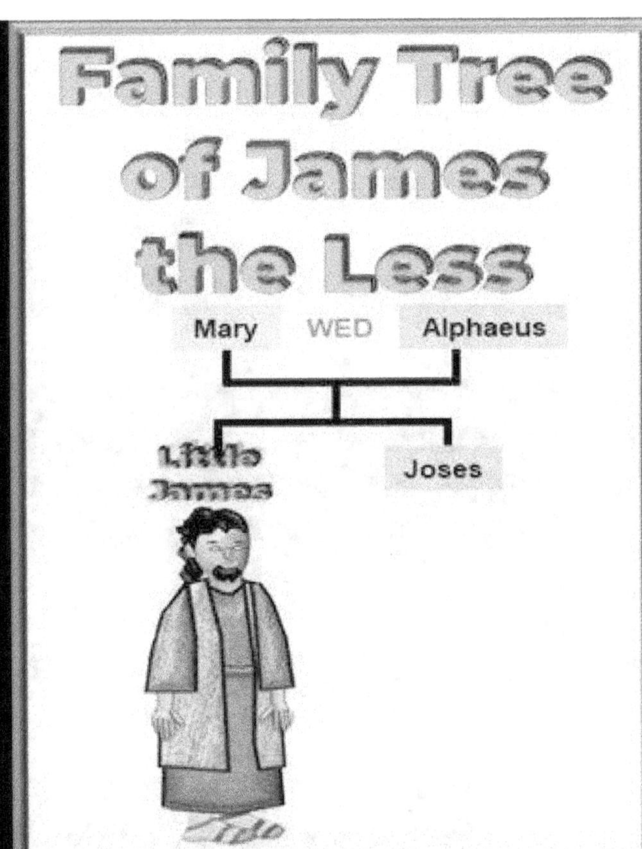

● **Mary Magdalene**	Matthew 27:56; Mark 15:40; John 19:25
● **Mary Mother of Jesus**	John 19:25
● **Disciple John Z.**	John 19:25
● **Salome:** wife of Zebedee, mother of Disciples James Z. and John Z.	Matthew 27:56; Mark 15:40
● **Mary:** wife of Cleophas, Sister-in-law to Mary	John 19:25
● **Mary:** wife of Alpheus, Mother of James the Less & his brother Joses	Matthew 27:56; Mark 15:40

REMEZ – Hidden Messages

King David prophesied & foreshadowed

KING JAMES VERSION BIBLE (KJV)
Psalm 22:17 I may tell all my bones: they look and stare upon me.

Prophet Isaiah prophesied & foreshadowed

Isaiah 52:2 … when we shall see him, there is no beauty that we should desire him.

Isaiah 52:3 He is despised and rejected of men; a man of sorrows, and acquainted with grief: and we hid as it were our faces from him; he was despised, and we esteemed him not.

Isaiah 52:4 Surely he hath borne our griefs, and carried our sorrows: yet we did esteem him stricken, smitten of God, and afflicted.

Isaiah 52:14 As many were astonied at thee; his visage was so marred more than any man, and his form more than the sons of men: 15 So shall he sprinkle many nations; the kings shall shut their mouths at him: for that which had not been told them shall they see; and that which they had not heard shall they consider.

Just as Prophesied in Old Testament, Jesus had no broken bones but was pierced in His side by soldiers.

7th of 7 WOWS after Jesus died on the Cross

BIBLE CLUES (KJV) ??? Examine 4 Gospels for Clues (KJV) ??? BIBLE CLUES (KJV)

John 19:31-37

31 The Jews therefore, because it was the preparation, that the bodies should not remain upon the cross on the sabbath day, (for that sabbath day was an high day,) besought Pilate that their legs might be broken, and that they might be taken away.

32 Then came the soldiers, and brake the legs of the first, and of the other which was crucified with him. 33 But when they came to Jesus, and saw that he was dead already, they brake not his legs: 34 But one of the soldiers with a spear pierced his side, and forthwith came there out blood and water.

35 And he that saw it bare record, and his record is true: and he knoweth that he saith true, that ye might believe. 36 For these things were done, that the scripture should be fulfilled, A bone of him shall not be broken. 37 And again another scripture saith, They shall look on him whom they pierced.

PIERCED - NOT BROKEN

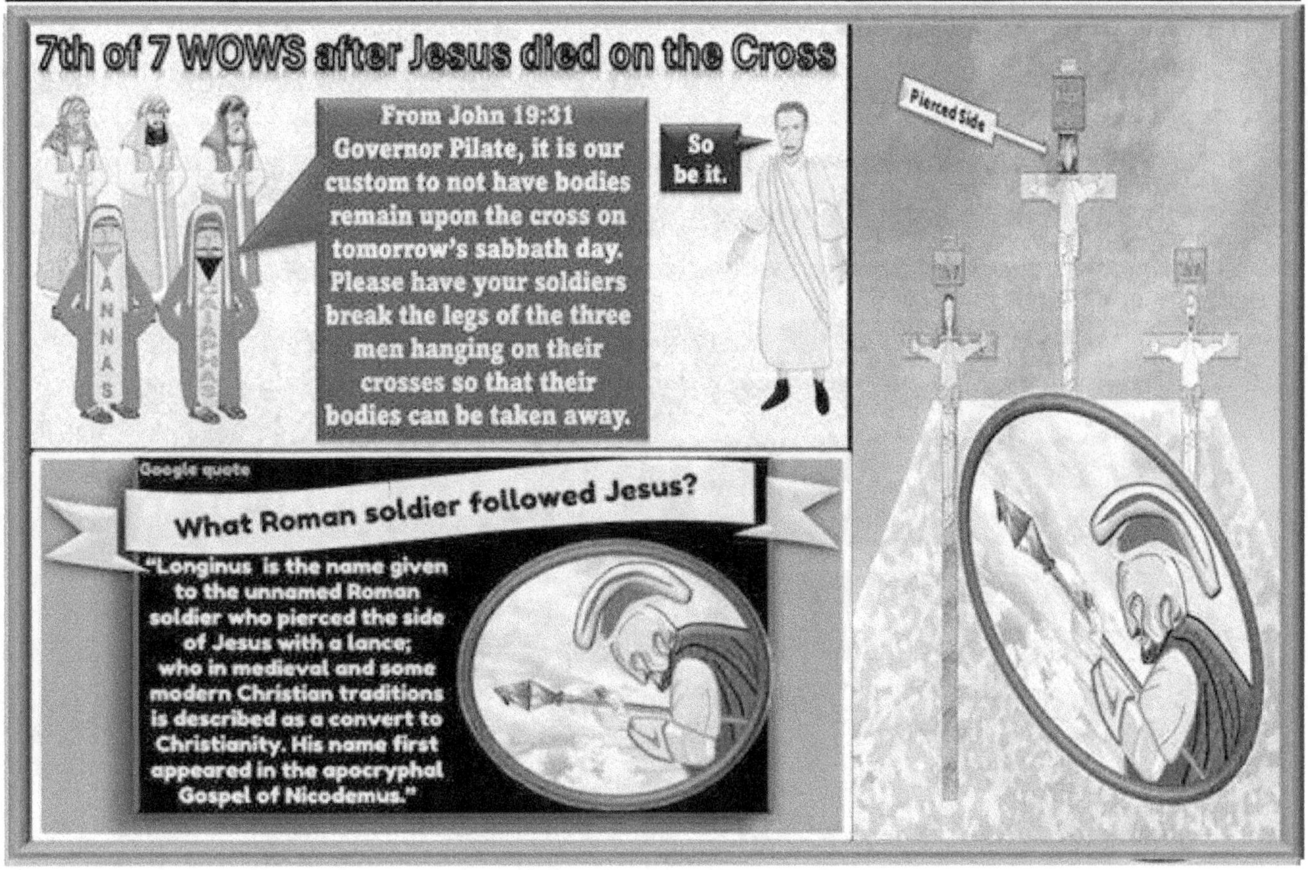

7th of 7 WOWS after Jesus died on the Cross

REMEZ – Hidden Messages
NO BROKEN BONES

King David **prophesied & foreshadowed**

Moses **prophesied & foreshadowed**

REMEZ – Hidden Messages
JESUS WAS PIERCED

KING JAMES VERSION BIBLE (KJV)
Psalm 22:14 I am poured out like water, and all my bones are out of joint: my heart is like wax; it is melted in the midst of my bowels. *FYI – Blood & water poured out from Jesus' side.*

Psalm 22:14 ... they pierced my hands and my feet.

Prophet Zechariah prophesied & foreshadowed

KING JAMES VERSION BIBLE (KJV)
Zechariah 12:10 And I will pour upon the house of David, and upon the inhabitants of Jerusalem, the spirit of grace and of supplications: and they shall look upon me whom they have pierced, and they shall mourn for him, as one mourneth for his only son, and shall be in bitterness for him, as one that is in bitterness for his firstborn.

REMEZ – Hidden Messages
JESUS WAS PIERCED
continued

Prophet Isaiah — prophesied & foreshadowed

KING JAMES VERSION BIBLE (KJV)

Isaiah 53:5 But he was wounded (i.e., PIERCED) for our transgressions, he was bruised for our iniquities: the chastisement of our peace was upon him; and with his stripes we are healed.

Isaiah 53:6 All we like sheep have gone astray; we have turned every one to his own way; and the Lord hath laid on him the iniquity of us all.

Isaiah 53:7 He was oppressed, and he was afflicted, yet he opened not his mouth: he is brought as a lamb to the slaughter, and as a sheep before her shearers is dumb, so he openeth not his mouth.

The Roman soldiers pierced Jesus' side but did not break His bones. There is much more to this part of the crucifixion than those two facts. It testifies to just how amazing our Triune God is. It also demonstrates how intentional each word of the Holy Bible is.

In mid-December 2023, my church put on a production called "*The Story of Christmas.*" One very touching detail included the '*word of knowledge*' that shepherds used swaddling strips of cloth to wrap the legs of lambs selected to be sacrificial lambs to prevent them from getting blemishes. Similarly, Mary wrapped baby Jesus in swaddling strips of cloth for three reasons:

1 **Doing so would help her baby make a smooth transition from the tight confines of her womb to being still wrapped and coddled as He made His transition into beginning His infant life.**

2 **It was the custom of the day to do this.**

3 **Baby Jesus was to grow up to be our sacrificial lamb.**

On the day Jesus came to be baptized, in **John 1:20**, John the Baptist confirmed this fact by announcing, "Look, the Lamb of God, who takes away the sin of the world!"

This declaration hails back to the Prophecies declared by Moses almost 1500 years before Jesus' birth. See the timeline on the next page.

At the beginning of the 40-year Exodus, God gave Moses precise instructions regarding how the Children of Israel were to prepare their Passover lamb. Moses recorded these instructions in the books of Exodus and Numbers. Little did he suspect that this was to be part of the Prophecy that would point to the crucifixion of Jesus about 1500 years later. In those instructions, God directed that nobody was allowed to break the bones of the sacrificial lamb. To fulfill the Prophecy, Jesus had to make sure He died before the Romans needed to hasten His death by breaking His legs.

Moses

4000 BC — Adam & Eve
3500 BC — Enoch was not during this stretch
3000 BC — Noah born
2500 BC — The Flood
Ocean Waters Unending
[Born 1948 BC] 2000 BC — Abraham
1500 BC — Moses
1000 BC — King David
King David
500 BC — King Zedekiah
JESUS
4 BC — Christ Jesus born
30 AD — Crucifixion & Resurrection
1030 AD — 1000 years since Res.
1948 AD — Israel Declared a Nation
2020 AD — Covid-19 Pandemic
2021 AD — 1991 years since Res.
2022 AD — 1992 years since Res.
2023 AD — 1993 years since Res.
2024 AD — November - US Elections
2025 AD — 1995 years since Res.
2026 AD — 1996 years since Res.
2027 AD — 1997 years since Res.
2028 AD — November - US Elections
2029 AD — 1999 years since Res.
2030 AD — 2000 years since Res.
2031 AD — 1st year of 3rd Millennium
2032 AD — 2nd year of 3rd Millennium
Second ??? Coming

PART 3: SOLDIERS PIERCED JESUS' SIDE BUT DID NOT BREAK HIS BONES

To appreciate what it means that Jesus died for our sins, we must comprehend how this tradition got started.

Disclaimer: Since I was brought up as a Christian and not a Jew, I had to do a bit of studying. Please forgive me if, through lack of knowledge, I am oversimplifying this process.

First, let's discuss the original meaning of **SIN**.

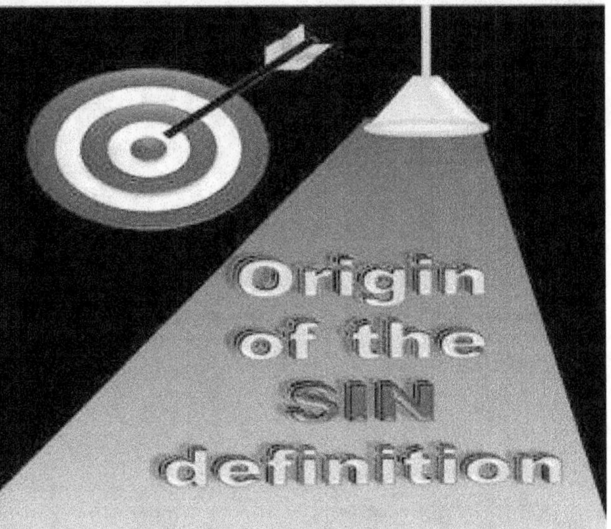

It certainly feels less humbling when we can say, "Oops! I missed the mark." as opposed to having to admit, "Oh, no! I sinned. Please forgive me!" Nevertheless, the Bible clearly states:

> **Ezekiel 18:20** The one who sins is the one who will die.

> **Romans 6:23** For the wages of sin is death, but the gift of God is eternal life in Christ Jesus our Lord.

 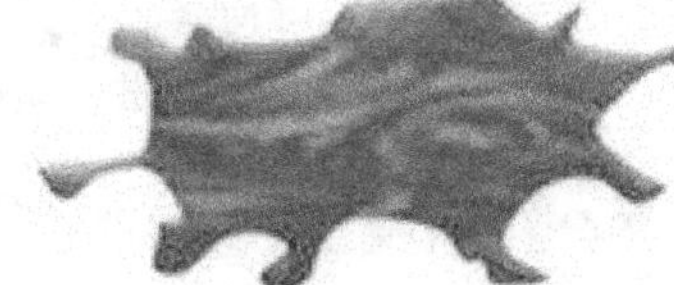 

> **Psalm 145:20** The Lord watches over all who love him, but all the wicked he will destroy.

> **Leviticus 17:11** For the life of a creature is in the blood, and I have given it to you to make atonement for yourselves on the altar; it is the blood that makes atonement for one's life.

In the Old Testament, Christ Jesus had not yet been born into an earthly life. So, since He was not available to give His life to atone for OUR sins, God had to find some legal way to get around having to kill all of His beloved children. Our Heavenly Father did not want to see them die. He also did not desire to send them to hell to live out their eternity with Satan, the demons, and the fallen angels.

So, God taught the following process to Moses. In turn, Moses taught this process to the Children of Israel.

Source: Synopsis of parts of Leviticus Chapters 1 to 6

STEP 4: The Israelite will sacrifice the lamb to become free of sin. Then, the priest will do this:

Lev 4:34 Then the priest shall take some of the blood of the sin offering with his finger and put it on the horns of the altar of burnt offering and pour out the rest of the blood at the base of the altar. (NIV)

Ever since Jesus was crucified, resurrected, and ascended to Heaven, accepting Him as your Lord and Savior is the ONLY way God will wipe you clean of your sins. Here is one of the many versions of a **SINNER'S PRAYER** you could choose to pray to be saved and redeemed by Jesus:

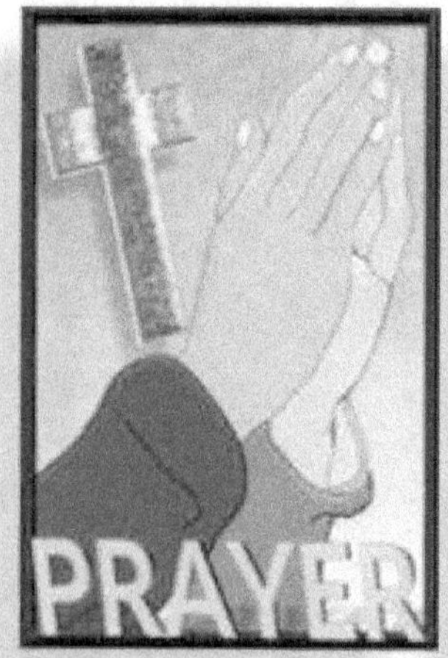

Dear Lord Jesus, I know that I am a sinner, and I ask for Your forgiveness. I believe You died for my sins and rose from the dead. I turn from my sins and invite You to come into my heart and life. I want to trust and follow You as my Lord and Savior. -- GOOGLE QUOTE

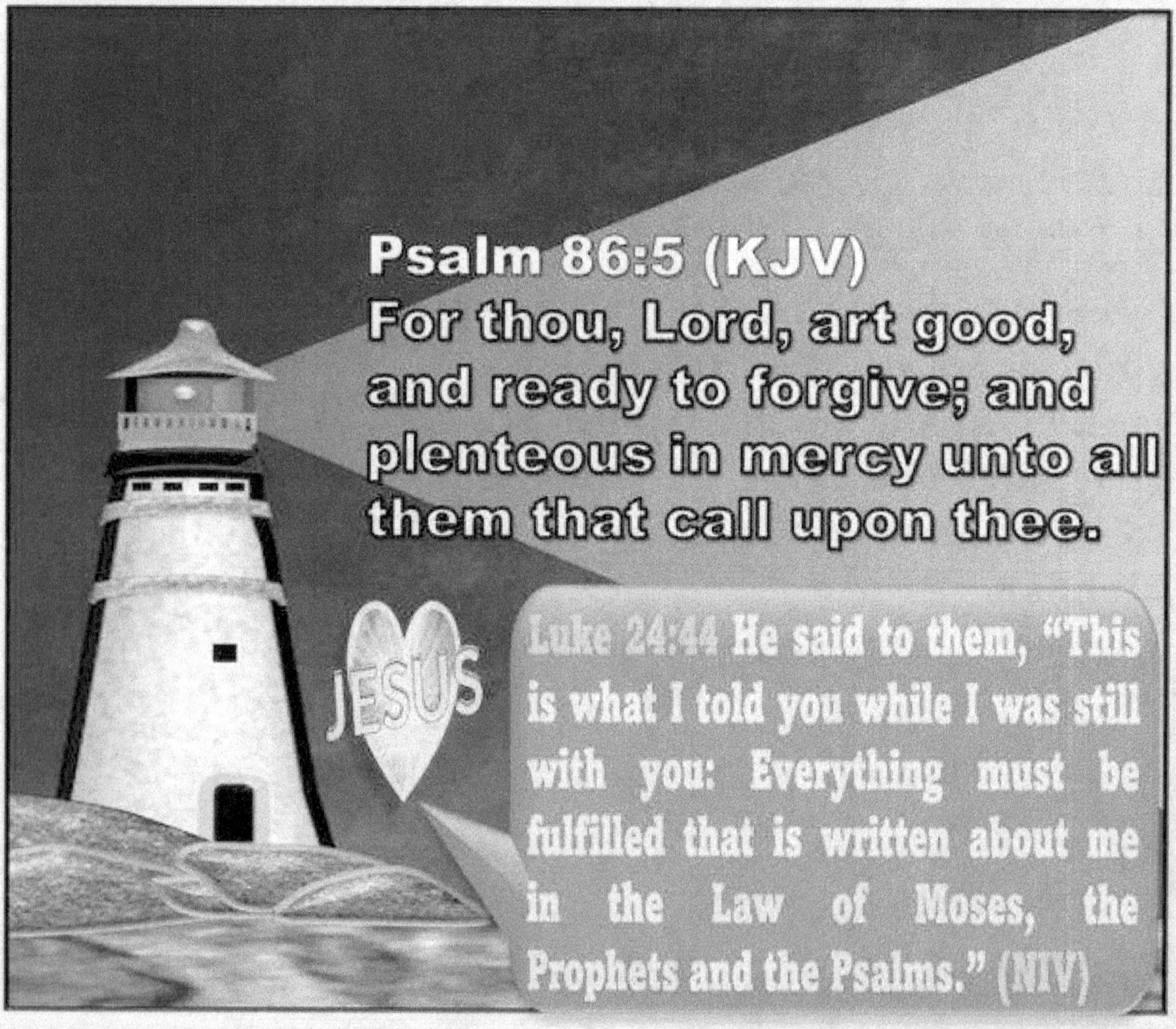

Consider this **THOUGHT EXPERIMENT**. Imagine that **God, His Son Jesus Christ, and the Holy Spirit** are orchestrating things for OUR GOOD behind the scenes. We still have the gift of our free will. But based on our actions, the **Trinity** will orchestrate things for our benefit so that we can live as closely as possible to **HIS PURPOSE** ordained for our lives. He will also arrange for **DIVINE APPOINTMENTS** with people who can teach us things, or we can teach things to them. We may be with these people only for short periods or seasons (i.e., mere seconds, minutes, hours, days, weeks, or months). Some people we will be with for years.

Now, let's take this **THOUGHT EXPERIMENT** a step further. **God** can see things happening simultaneously: Past, present, and future. So, when He gave instructions to Moses to share with the Children of Israel, He could also make some of those directions be Prophecies that **His Son** would replicate when he arrived in Galilee about 4 BC and was crucified, at the age of 33, about 30 AD.

God is the great Orchestrator!

Why was that important? Part of the proof or validation for the Temple elders and the Hebrew people that Jesus was indeed that promised Messiah was Him fulfilling most, if not all, of the Old Testament Prophecies.

Jesus would get up early every morning to spend time with His Father and the Holy Spirit. These daily prayer gatherings would be similar to a General meeting with his high-level consultants planning every move they would make on any given day. Jesus said: See next page.

As you know, in the Garden of Gethsemane, when Jesus went alone to pray, He begged God to reveal an alternate way to save all humans that would not involve Him suffering such unbearable pain. He was so terrified that He was literally sweating blood. What a blessing that His Father sent an angel to comfort Him. When His Father confirmed that this was the only legal way to release humans from suffering eternal torment in hell, Jesus stated in **Matthew 26:42,** "May your will be done." In other words, Jesus' Love for us far exceeded His fear and dread.

In my imagination, I picture God reminding Jesus of the remaining unfulfilled Prophesies that the Trinity had strategized more than 1500 years ago. For example, He might have said, "Remember, my beloved Son, you cannot die before 3 PM, but you must die very soon after so that the Roman soldiers won't break your bones to hasten your death."

They would recall the Prophesies they provided to Moses and King David.

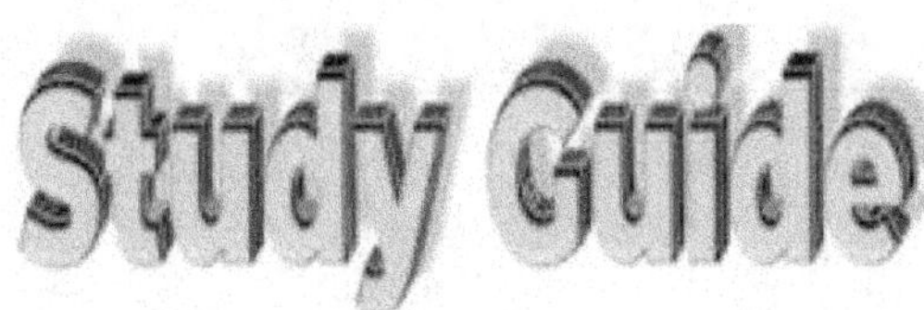

1. For the **first Wow**, describe your understanding of why Jesus was able to die on command.

2. For the **second Wow**, describe what happened with the veil splitting. How does that impact our present-day lives?

3. In your opinion, what do you think the High Priest, Caiaphas, was thinking when he witnessed the veil splitting from top to bottom?

4. Describe in what ways the Sanhedrin broke the Ten Commandments the week leading up to Jesus' death and the day of His death.

5. For the **third Wow**, describe where you think the earthquake hit the hardest and why.

6. Why is it important that we don't hold grudges against other people, including people we read about in the Bible?

7. For the **fourth Wow**, describe your theory about the people whose tombs broke open and who came back to life.

8. For the **fifth Wow**, which of the Roman soldiers do you think decided that Jesus must be the Son of God? Do you think he or they will secretly become a Christian?

9. For the **sixth Wow**, what do you think was going through the minds of the people who viewed Jesus' corpse after He died?

10. Look through the Remez Bible verses mentioned in these last few chapters. Which one or ones impact you the most? Please explain.

11. For the **seventh Wow**, why do you think it was important that Jesus' bones were not broken?

12. Why do you think a combination of blood and water poured out of Jesus' body when the Roman soldier pierced His dead body?

13. What are some of the key factors you notice about the timeline that is located between Chapter 9 and 10 on page 42?

14. Give one or more examples of ways you feel like Almighty God has orchestrated things in your life for your benefit.

PILATE PERMITTED JOSEPH OF ARIMATHEA TO HOUSE JESUS' BODY IN HIS TOMB.

Matthew 27:57 As evening approached, there came a rich man from Arimathea, named Joseph, who had himself become a disciple of Jesus. **58 Going to Pilate,** he asked for Jesus' body, **and Pilate ordered that it be given to him. (NIV)**

Who was Joseph of Arimathea?

From **Matthew 27:57**, **Mark 15:53**, **Luke 23:50-51**, and **John 19:38**, we learn:

- He was a rich man from Arimathea, a city of the Jews.

- He was a secret disciple of Jesus.

- He was an honorable counselor.

- He was a good man and just.

- He was a member of the Sanhedrin.

- We learn in **John 19:38**, for fear of the Sanhedrin, Joseph secretly went to Pilate to request permission to bury Jesus in his own tomb.

- We learn in **Luke 23:51** that he had not consented to the Sanhedrin counsel who voted for Jesus to die.

Jesus was laid in a Rich Man's Tomb on Friday

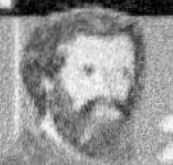

Examine 4 Gospels for Clues (KJV)

Matthew 27:57-60	Mark 15:42-46	Luke 23:50-54	John 19:38-42
57 When the even was come, there came a rich man of Arimathaea, named Joseph, who also himself was Jesus' disciple: **58** He went to Pilate, and begged the body of Jesus. Then Pilate commanded the body to be delivered. **59** And when Joseph had taken the body, he wrapped it in a clean linen cloth, **60** And laid it in his own new tomb, which he had hewn out in the rock: and he rolled a great stone to the door of the sepulcher, and departed.	**42** And now when the even was come, because it was the preparation, that is, the day before the sabbath, **43** Joseph of Arimathaea, an honourable counsellor, which also waited for the kingdom of God, came, and went in boldly unto Pilate, and craved the body of Jesus. **44** And Pilate marvelled if he were already dead: and calling unto him the centurion, he asked him whether he had been any while dead. **45** And when he knew it of the centurion, he gave the body to Joseph. **46** And he bought fine linen, and took him down, and wrapped him in the linen, and laid him in a sepulchre which was hewn out of a rock, and rolled a stone unto the door of the sepulchre.	**50** And, behold, there was a man named Joseph, a counsellor; and he was a good man, and a just: **51** (The same had not consented to the counsel and deed of them;) he was of Arimathaea, a city of the Jews: who also himself waited for the kingdom of God. **52** This man went unto Pilate, and begged the body of Jesus. **53** And he took it down, and wrapped it in linen, and laid it in a sepulchre that was hewn in stone, wherein never man before was laid. **54** And that day was the preparation, and the sabbath drew on.	**38** And after this Joseph of Arimathaea, being a disciple of Jesus, but secretly for fear of the Jews, besought Pilate that he might take away the body of Jesus: and Pilate gave him leave. He came therefore, and took the body of Jesus. **39** And there came also Nicodemus, which at the first came to Jesus by night, and brought a mixture of myrrh and aloes, about an hundred pound weight. **40** Then took they the body of Jesus, and wound it in linen clothes with the spices, as the manner of the Jews is to bury. **41** Now in the place where he was crucified there was a garden; and in the garden a new sepulchre, wherein was never man yet laid. **42** There laid they Jesus therefore because of the Jews' preparation day; for the sepulchre was nigh at hand.

Jesus was laid in a Rich Man's Tomb on Friday

continued

Examine 4 Gospels for Clues (KJV)

Matthew 27:61	Mark 15:47	Luke 23:55-56	John
61 And there was Mary Magdalene, and the other Mary, sitting over against the sepulcher.	47 And Mary Magdalene and Mary the mother of Joses beheld where he was laid.	55 And the women also, which came with him from Galilee, followed after, and beheld the sepulchre, and how his body was laid. 56 And they returned, and prepared spices and ointments; and rested the sabbath day according to the commandment.	No Reference to this Topic.

The other Mary was likely the aunt of Jesus.

REMEZ – Hidden Messages
RICH MAN'S TOMB
Prophet Isaiah prophesied & foreshadowed

KING JAMES VERSION BIBLE (KJV)

Isaiah 53:8 He was taken from prison and from judgment: and who shall declare his generation? for he was cut off out of the land of the living: for the transgression of my people was he stricken.

Isaiah 53:9 And he made his grave with the wicked, and with the rich in his death; because he had done no violence, neither was any deceit in his mouth.

Isaiah 53:10 Yet it pleased the Lord to bruise him; he hath put him to grief: when thou shalt make his soul an offering for sin, he shall see his seed, he shall prolong his days, and the pleasure of the Lord shall prosper in his hand.

Isaiah 53:11 He shall see of the travail of his soul, and shall be satisfied: by his knowledge shall my righteous servant justify many; for he shall bear their iniquities.

Isaiah 53:12 Therefore will I divide him a portion with the great, and he shall divide the spoil with the strong; because he hath poured out his soul unto death: and he was numbered with the transgressors; and he bare the sin of many, and made intercession for the transgressors.

Until that day of Jesus' crucifixion, two members of the Sanhedrin, Joseph of Arimathea and Nicodemus, were too afraid to lose their favored spot in the Sanhedrin. Consider this:

To the benefit of their salvation, these two men had a change of heart. We can only speculate if the ruling members of the Sanhedrin decided to kick them out. The Bible does not reveal that answer.

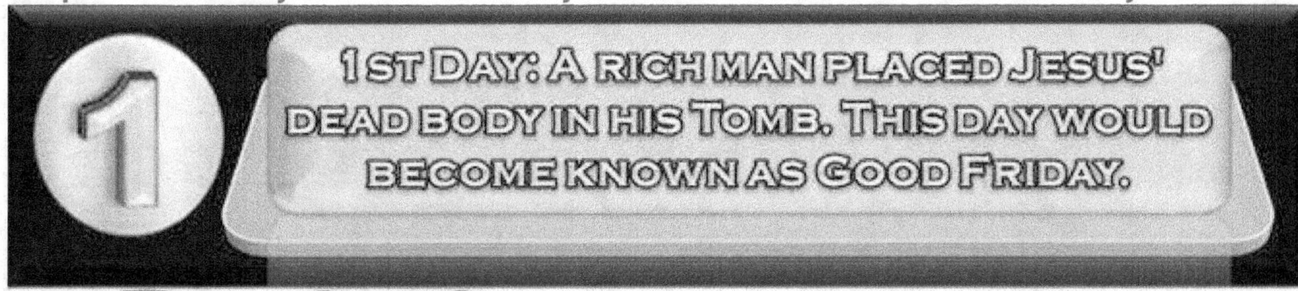

Jesus Christ died very soon after it turned 3 PM on Friday. According to Jewish tradition, Jesus' body must be taken down from the cross and placed inside an enclosed tomb before sunset. So, during that 3-hour interval, rich man Joseph Arimathea had to get special permission from Pilate to remove His body from the cross, get Him inside his unused tomb, prepare Him for burial, roll the stone to seal off the tomb, and return to his own home, all before 6 PM. We learn in **John 19:39** that Pharisee Nicodemus, another secret follower of Christ, assisted him.

REMEZ –
Hidden Messages prophesied & foreshadowed

KING JAMES VERSION BIBLE (KJV)
Deuteronomy 21:23 His body shall not remain all night upon the tree, but thou shalt in any wise bury him that day; (for he that is hanged is accursed of God;) that thy land be not defiled, which the Lord thy God giveth thee for an inheritance.

Galatians 3:13 Christ hath redeemed us from the curse of the law, being made a curse for us: for it is written, Cursed is every one that hangeth on a tree: 14 That the blessing of Abraham might come on the Gentiles through Jesus Christ; that we might receive the promise of the Spirit through faith.

Prophet Jeremiah

KING JAMES VERSION BIBLE (KJV)
Jeremiah 11:19 But I was like a lamb or an ox that is brought to the slaughter; and I knew not that they had devised devices against me, saying, Let us destroy the tree with the fruit thereof, and let us cut him off from the land of the living, that his name may be no more remembered.

While Jesus' dead body lay in the tomb between sunset on Friday and before dawn on Sunday, where did the spirit of Jesus go?

From **Matthew 12:38-42**, you may recall that the Scribes and the Pharisees challenged Jesus to show them a sign to prove that He was indeed the promised Messiah.

Instead of giving in to their request, Jesus stated, in **verse 39**, "An evil and adulterous generation seeketh after a sign; and there shall no sign be given to it, but the sign of the prophet Jonas: 40 For as Jonas was three days and three nights in the whale's belly; so shall the Son of man be three days and three nights in the heart of the earth. 41 The men of Nineveh shall rise in judgment with this generation, and shall condemn it: because they repented at the preaching of Jonas; and, behold, a greater than Jonas is here. 42 The queen of the south shall rise up in the judgment with this generation, and shall condemn it: for she came from the uttermost parts of the earth to hear the wisdom of Solomon; and, behold, a greater than Solomon is here." (This encounter was also referenced in **Matthew 16:1-4** and **Luke 11:29-30**.)

*(FYI – the queen of the south was the Queen of Sheba who came to meet with King Solomon. **1 Kings 10:1–29**.*

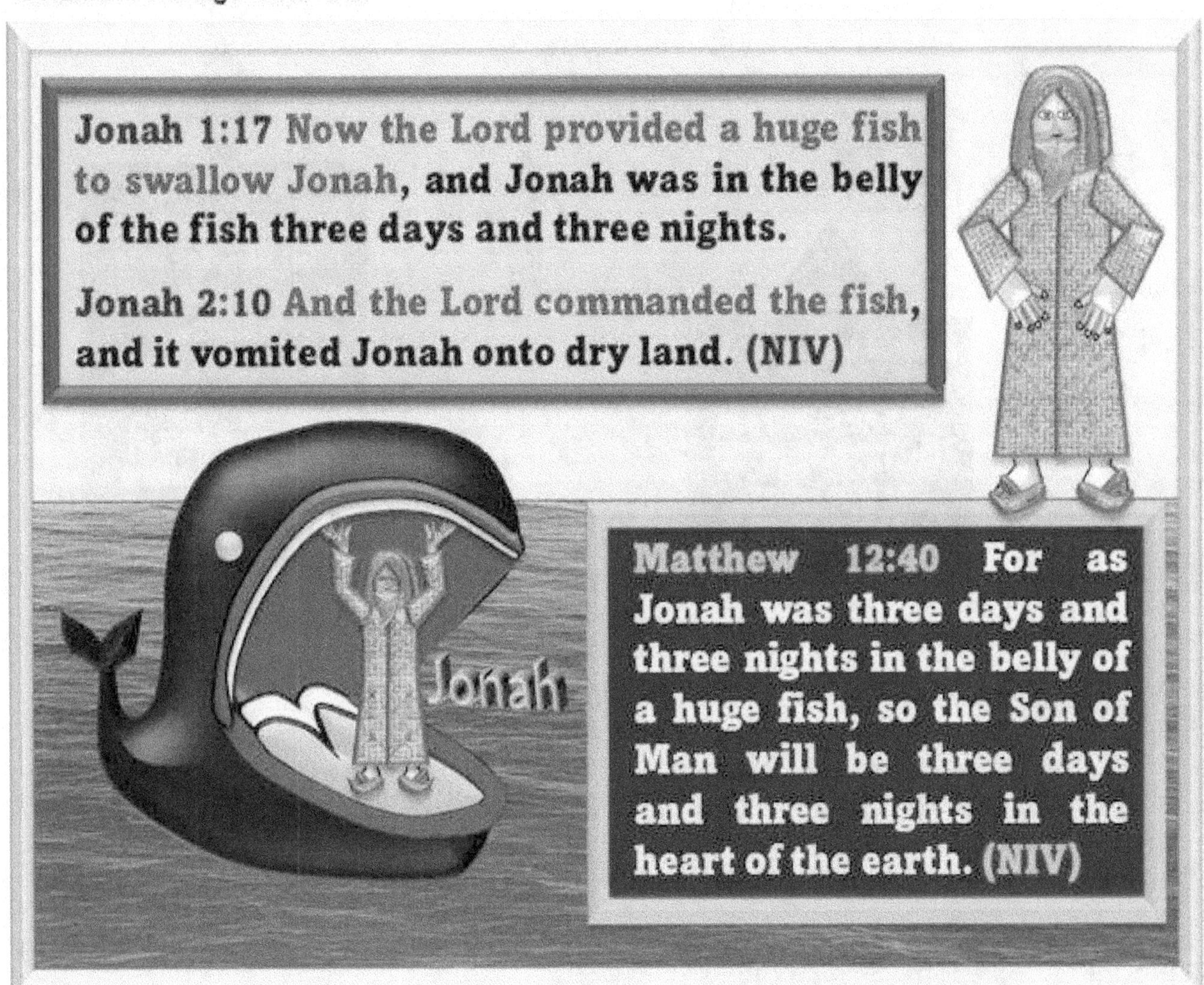

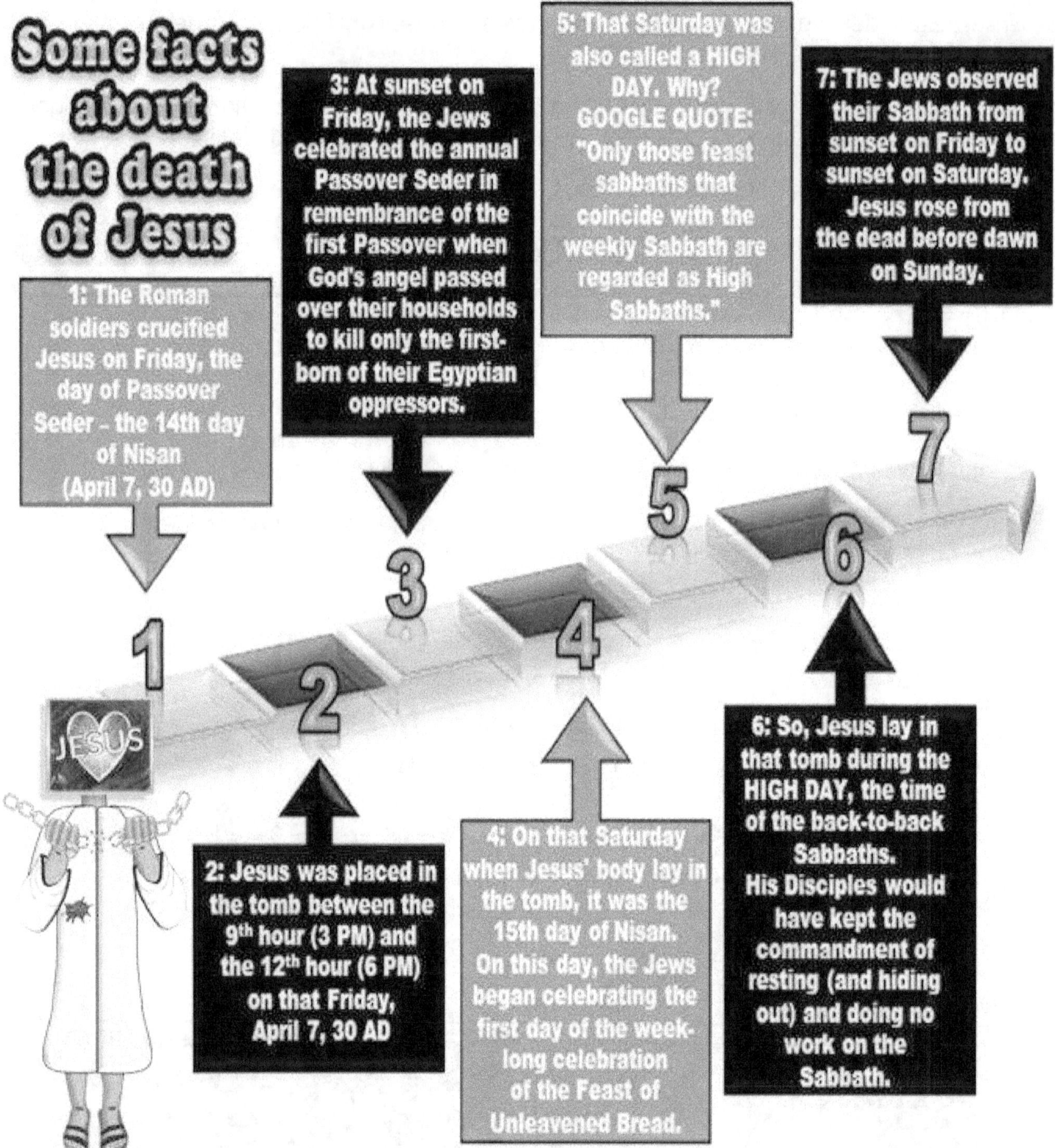

Who was in power during the Life and Crucifixion of Jesus?

1) Roman Emperor Tiberius reigned from 14 AD to 37 AD.
2) Pontius Pilate was prefect (governor) of Judaea from 26 AD 26 to 36 AD.
3) Caiaphas was high priest in Jerusalem from 18 AD to 36 AD.
4) Herod Antipas was tetrarch of Galilee from 4 BC to 39 AD.
5) Herod the Great was king of Judea from 37 BC to March or April 4 BC.

Jesus was crucified on the 14th day of Nisan which was April 7, 30 AD. Jesus was thought to be about 33 years old.

How do we explain that Jesus was in tomb for less than 72 hours?

Mark 8:31 And he began to teach them, that the Son of man must suffer many things, and be rejected of the elders, and of the chief priests, and scribes, and be killed, and after three days rise again.

Mark 9:31 For he taught his disciples, and said unto them, The Son of man is delivered into the hands of men, and they shall kill him; and after that he is killed, he shall rise the third day.

John 2:19 Jesus answered and said unto them, Destroy this temple, and in three days I will raise it up.

John 2:20 Then said the Jews, Forty and six years was this temple in building, and wilt thou rear it up in three days?

John 2:21 But he spake of the temple of his body.

John 2:22 When therefore he was risen from the dead, his disciples remembered that he had said this unto them; and they believed the scripture, and the word which Jesus had said. (KJV)

Bible Info.com quote

How do we justify the time Jesus spent in the tomb since it was less than 72 hours?

"In studying this problem, we need to bear in mind that Jesus was born and raised in the East under the influence of Eastern customs and language. He used the idioms of His time and country and was accustomed to using the Jewish method of determining time.

Part of Friday = 1 day/night PLUS All of Saturday = 1 day/night PLUS Part of Sunday = 1 day/night. All of this is the equivalent of 3 days and 3 nights in the tomb.

'It is to be observed that the Jews and other Orientals generally speak of any part of a day, or a period of time as if it were the whole. In like manner, fractions of a day are in England treated as legally whole days.' ... 'The Son of man shall be three 'onahs' in the heart of the earth. 'Onah' meant a day and a night, and a part of an 'onah' was reckoned as a whole.'"

When did Jesus begin His ministry?

Luke 3:23 Now Jesus himself was about thirty years old when he began his ministry. He was the son, so it was thought, of Joseph, the son of Heli, 24 the son of Matthat, … (NIV)

When was Jesus born? Although there is controversy, several scholars agree that Jesus was born in 4 BC. Some say it might have been as early as 6 or 7 BC, and some state it might have been as late as 1 BC. For the sake of simplicity, this book lists His birth year as 4 BC.

How do we explain the timing of the census mentioned in Luke 2:1-7?

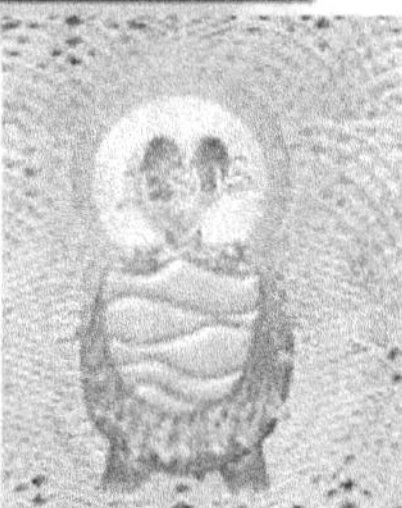

Luke 2:1 And it came to pass in those days, that there went out a decree from Caesar Augustus that all the world should be taxed.

Luke 2:2 (And this taxing was first made when Cyrenius was governor of Syria.) [GOOGLE QUOTE: Publius Sulpicius Quirinius (c. 51 BC – AD 21), also translated as Cyrenius, was a Roman aristocrat.]

Luke 2:3 And all went to be taxed, every one into his own city. 4 And Joseph also went up from Galilee, out of the city of Nazareth, into Judaea, unto the city of David, which is called Bethlehem; (because he was of the house and lineage of David:) 5 To be taxed with Mary his espoused wife, being great with child.

Luke 2:6 And so it was, that, while they were there, the days were accomplished that she should be delivered. 7 And she brought forth her firstborn son, and wrapped him in swaddling clothes, and laid him in a manger; because there was no room for them in the inn. (KJV)

CENSUS DETAILS

How do we explain the timing of the census?

"Many censuses were taken in the Roman empire during the time of Augustus, and there is no reason why Herod might not have been asked to take one, especially in light of conditions near the end of his life. Since censuses were carried out locally, local customs were regarded and Palestine was a delicate area.

Quirinius may or may not have been governor of Syria at the birth of Christ in 5 B.C., but this is irrelevant since Luke 2:2 states that the census during which Jesus was born was the first one, before the more well-known one taken by Quirinius in A.D. 6-7. This first one was "in the days of Herod the king."

-- Quote from Wayne Brindle for Liberty University.

More about the timing of the census:

"Whether Quirinius was governor when Jesus was born is a moot point; he evidently was in a position of authority at the time. There are two concluding points to be considered:

1. At the command of Quirinius of Syria, the first census was taken while Herod the Great was still king. Rome knew all too well of Herod's health issues, that he was a brutal dictator, and there was always imminent danger of a rebellion. They were not about to take any chances in this volatile part of the world. The death of Herod the Great and the rivalry of his sons that followed provided ample opportunity for another Jewish revolt.

2. The first census was taken before the more well-known census which was also issued by the same Quirinius. Augustus may have wanted the census to be taken gradually as not to stir an uprising.

... Luke did not record the name of the official political governor of Syria, but rather, recorded the name of the acting governor who held temporary rulership. He initiated the census and reported directly to the emperor himself. For this reason, Joseph had to take Mary and travel to his ancestral village of Bethlehem." **-- Quote from Bill Heinrich for Mysteries of the Messiah.**

2ND DAY: ON SATURDAY, AS THE DISCIPLES HIDE AND CRY, JESUS' DEAD BODY IS STILL IN THAT LONELY TOMB.

Matthew 27:62 Now the next day, that followed the day of the preparation, the chief priests and Pharisees came together unto Pilate, **63** Saying, Sir, we remember that that deceiver said, while he was yet alive, After three days I will rise again.

Matthew 27:64 Command therefore that the sepulchre be made sure until the third day, lest his disciples come by night, and steal him away, and say unto the people, He is risen from the dead: so the last error shall be worse than the first.

Matthew 27:65 Pilate said unto them, Ye have a watch: go your way, make it as sure as ye can.

Matthew 27:66 So they went, and made the sepulchre sure, sealing the stone, and setting a watch. (KJV)

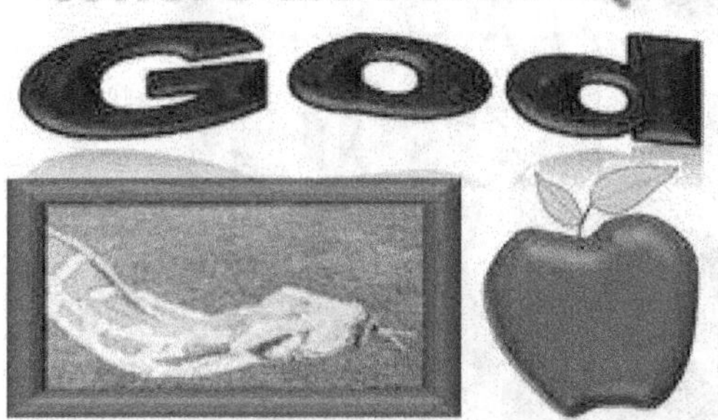

> **Genesis 3:15 And I will put enmity between thee and the woman, and between thy seed and her seed; it shall bruise thy head, and thou shalt bruise his heel. (KJV)**

Since Moses penned the '*God-breathed*' verse, **Genesis 3:15**, we have known that Christ Jesus would fulfill this Prophecy by His crucifixion on the Cross and His resurrection from the tomb.

So, where did Jesus' spirit go between the crucifixion and resurrection? Notice what it states in the APOSTLES' CREED quoted below:

FYI – There was no offense intended to this beautiful Indian Python.

Google quote plus quote by USCCB

Apostles' Creed

"What churches use the Apostle creed in worship? It has been used in the Latin liturgical rites since the 8th century and, by extension, in the various modern branches of Western Christianity, including the modern liturgy and catechesis of the Catholic Church, Lutheranism, Anglicanism, Presbyterianism, Moravianism, Methodism, and Congregational churches."

Apostles' Creed

I believe in God, the Father almighty,
Creator of heaven and earth,
and in Jesus Christ, his only Son, our Lord,
who was conceived by the Holy Spirit,
born of the Virgin Mary,
suffered under Pontius Pilate,
was crucified, died and was buried;
he descended into hell;
on the third day he rose again from the dead;
he ascended into heaven,
and is seated at the right hand of God the Father almighty;
from there he will come to judge the living and the dead.

I believe in the Holy Spirit, the holy catholic Church,
the communion of saints, the forgiveness of sins,
the resurrection of the body, and life everlasting. Amen.

What does the Old Testament call hell?

"Biblical terminology: Sheol
In the King James Bible, the Old Testament term Sheol is translated as "Hell" 31 times, and it is translated as "the grave" 31 times. Sheol is also translated as "the pit" three times."

What does the New Testament call hell?

"Biblical terminology: Hades
Different Hebrew and Greek words are translated as "Hell" in most English-language Bibles. These words include: "Sheol" in the Hebrew Bible, and "Hades" in the New Testament."

Is sheol the same as hell in the Bible?

"Usually Sheol was thought of 'as being deep down in the earth, as hell is often thought of today. In Old Testament Sheol is represented as the opposite of the upper sphere of life and light. It is "deep Sheol." It's direction is "down." The Psalmist says, "Thou hast delivered my soul from the lowest Sheol" (Ps. 86:13)."

In **Luke 16:19-31**, Jesus gives us a defining example of what might have occurred in hell before His crucifixion and resurrection. It is the story of a rich man who lived a selfish life and a beggar named Lazarus who lived a poor and deprived life. (*This is not the same Lazarus that Jesus raised from the dead.*)

Luke 16:19 There was a rich man who was dressed in purple and fine linen and lived in luxury every day.

Luke 16:20 At his gate was laid a beggar named Lazarus, covered with sores 21 and longing to eat what fell from the rich man's table. Even the dogs came and licked his sores.

Luke 16:22 The time came when the beggar died and the angels carried him to Abraham's side. The rich man also died and was buried.

Luke 16:23 In Hades, where he was in torment, he looked up and saw Abraham far away, with Lazarus by his side.

Luke 16:24 So he called to him, 'Father Abraham, have pity on me and send Lazarus to dip the tip of his finger in water and cool my tongue, because I am in agony in this fire.'

Luke 16:25 But Abraham replied, 'Son, remember that in your lifetime you received your good things, while Lazarus received bad things, but now he is comforted here and you are in agony.

Luke 16:26 And besides all this, between us and you a great chasm has been set in place, so that those who want to go from here to you cannot, nor can anyone cross over from there to us.'   CONTINUED →

Luke 16:27 **He answered, 'Then I beg you, Father, send Lazarus to my family, 28 for I have five brothers. Let him warn them, so that they will not also come to this place of torment.'**

Luke 16:29 **Abraham replied, 'They have Moses and the Prophets; let them listen to them.'**

Luke 16:30 **'No, Father Abraham,'** he said, **'but if someone from the dead goes to them, they will repent.'**

Luke 16:31 **He said to him, 'If they do not listen to Moses and the Prophets, they will not be convinced even if someone rises from the dead.'**

A supposition we might make is that since Jesus had not yet lived a sinless, earthly life and then died for our sins, King David, the Prophets, and other good people could not yet go straight to the Third Heaven to spend eternity with the Triune God: God the Father, God the Son, and God the Holy Spirit. Instead, they went to the good side of Hades, known as '**Abraham's bosom**,' to wait until Jesus would appear to lead them into Heaven.

JESUS
PAID IN FULL
Drunk & Disorderly
Cheating Financially
Extreme Anger
Mistreating Old People
Alcohol Abuse
Hatred
Revenge
Stalkers
DUI's
Unfair Wages
Abuse Spouse
Extortion
Trespassing
Snooping
Robbery
Usury
JESUS
Hypersensitivity
Stubbornness
Irresponsibility
Thoughtlessness
Cutting your body
Purposely hurtful
Bite Others
Hitting others
Exploit others
Pride
Alcohol Abuse
Extreme Anger
Kidnapping
Issuing Threats
Angry Outbursts
Temper Tantrums
Defrauding Others
Procrastination
Being Judgmental
Refusing to Forgive
Hating God
Ridiculing God
Denying God
Cursing God
Envy & Coveting
Mean Sarcasm
Cursing
Interrupting
Whining
False Flattery
Complaining
Excuse-making
Arrogance
Stalkers
Haters
Unfair Wages
Usury
Avarice
Indifference
Self-pity
Hypocrite
Self-righteous
Troublemaker
Laziness
Greed
Bullying
Persecution
Defiance
Malice
Being Cruel
Cheating on Tests
Mistreating Parents
Spiritual Sloth (Acedia)
Damaging people's property
Gluttony
Child Abuse
DUI's
Guilt
Trespassing
Bitterness
Extortion
Snooping
Robbery
Revenge
Gluttony
Drug Abuse
Child Abuse
Abuse Spouse
Vengeance
Mean Pranks
Envy
Selfishness
Ingratitude
Disrespectful
Jealousy
Power Lust
Money Lust
Insolence
Impatience
Prejudice
Drug Abuse
Defrauding Others
Disobedience
Cowardice
Idolatry
Divination
Sorcery
Occult Activities
Satanic Acts
Speak to Demons
Mind Control
Peer Pressure
Sacrilege
Atheism
Blasphemy
Being Rude
False Oaths
Lying
Gossip
Adulation
Heresy
Maligning
Boasting
Being Critical
Racism
Holding Grudges
Accidental Sin
Harm Handicapped People
Gas-lighter to Control Others
Psychological Warfare
Brainwash Others
Annoyed by Other's Successes
Skimp on your paid work
Justifying Wrong Attitudes
Making fun of People who Pray
Yelling & Screaming in mean way
Causing Physical Harm
Causing Emotional Harm
Undress people with your eyes
Calling people negative names
Kicking Others
Pinching Others
Fighting
Mob Mentality
Cheating Financially
Drunk & Disorderly
Being Lukewarm for God
Use Weapons to Harm Others
Perjury & False Witnesses
Take advantage of Poor
Meanly Argumentative
Mistreating Old People
Heckling a speaker
Jesus atoned for over 100 TRILLION sins committed by humans.

What does the Bible say where Jesus went?

Psalm 16:10 For thou wilt not leave my soul in hell; neither wilt thou suffer thine Holy One to see corruption. 11 Thou wilt shew me the path of life: in thy presence is fulness of joy; at thy right hand there are pleasures for evermore. (KJV)

Luke, who wrote the Book of Luke and at least the first part of Acts, echoed what King David said in the following verses:

Acts 2:27 Because thou wilt not leave my soul in hell, neither wilt thou suffer thine Holy One to see corruption.

Acts 2:28 Thou hast made known to me the ways of life; thou shalt make me full of joy with thy countenance. 29 Men and brethren, let me freely speak unto you of the patriarch David, that he is both dead and buried, and his sepulchre is with us unto this day.

Acts 2:30 Therefore being a prophet, and knowing that God had sworn with an oath to him, that of the fruit of his loins, according to the flesh, he would raise up Christ to sit on his throne; 31 He seeing this before spake of the resurrection of Christ, that his soul was not left in hell, neither his flesh did see corruption.

Acts 2:32 This Jesus hath God raised up, whereof we all are witnesses. 33 Therefore being by the right hand of God exalted, and having received of the Father the promise of the Holy Ghost, he hath shed forth this, which ye now see and hear.

Acts 2:34 For David is not ascended into the heavens: but he saith himself, The Lord said unto my Lord, Sit thou on my right hand, 35 Until I make thy foes thy footstool. 36 Therefore let all the house of Israel know assuredly, that God hath made the same Jesus, whom ye have crucified, both Lord and Christ. (KJV)

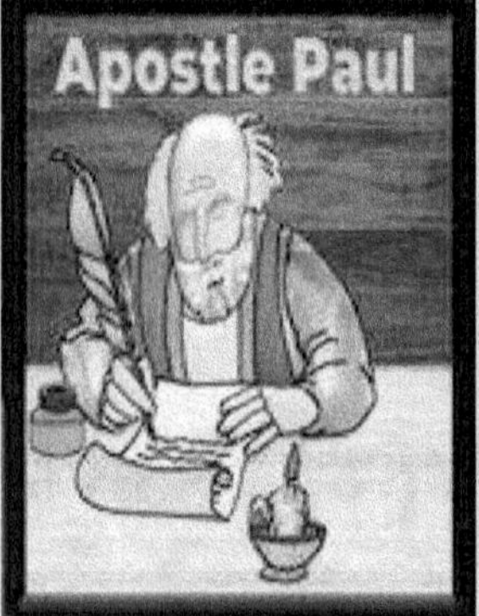

Ephesians 4:8 Wherefore he saith, When he ascended up on high, he led captivity captive, and gave gifts unto men.

9 (Now that he ascended, what is it but that he also descended first into the lower parts of the earth? 10 He that descended is the same also that ascended up far above all heavens, that he might fill all things.) (KJV)

1 Corinthians 15:20 But now is Christ risen from the dead, and become the firstfruits of them that slept. 21 For since by man came death, by man came also the resurrection of the dead. 22 For as in Adam all die, even so in Christ shall all be made alive. 23 But every man in his own order: Christ the firstfruits; afterward they that are Christ's at his coming. (KJV)

These next verses were penned by Peter or dictated by him about his memories. They imply that Jesus went to preach to those who died from drowning during the time of Noah.

1 Peter 3:18 For Christ also hath once suffered for sins, the just for the unjust, that he might bring us to God, being put to death in the flesh, but quickened by the Spirit: 19 By which also he went and preached unto the spirits in prison; 20 Which sometime were disobedient, when once the longsuffering of God waited in the days of Noah, while the ark was a preparing, wherein few, that is, eight souls were saved by water. (KJV)

1 Peter 4:5 Who shall give account to him that is ready to judge the quick and the dead.

1 Peter 4:6 For this cause was the gospel preached also to them that are dead, that they might be judged according to men in the flesh, but live according to God in the spirit. (KJV)

Did Jesus go to Hell? One possible answer.

"As Jesus neared death, He said, "It is finished" (John 19:30). His suffering in our place was completed. His soul/spirit went to hades (the place of the dead). Jesus did not go to "hell" or the suffering side of hades; He went to "Abraham's side" or the blessed side of hades. Jesus' suffering ended the moment He died. The payment for sin was paid. He then awaited the resurrection of His body and His return to glory in His ascension. Did Jesus go to hell? No. Did Jesus go to sheol/hades? Yes."

Did Jesus go to Hell? Another possible answer.

"To sum it up, before the resurrection of Jesus everyone went down to sheol (the realm of the dead) awaiting the death, burial, and resurrection of God's Son. The lost went to Hades where they will continue being tormented until the Great White Throne judgment (Revelation 20:11-14). The saved went to a place of comfort called Paradise (also known as Abraham's bosom). They could not go straight to heaven, into the presence of God, until the blood of Jesus had been shed to pay for and cover their sin. Thus Jesus Christ is the "firstfruits" of the dead (1 Corinthians 15:20).

But now is Christ risen from the dead, and become the firstfruits of them that slept. For since by man came death, by man came also the resurrection of the dead. For as in Adam all die, even so in Christ shall all be made alive. But every man in his own order: Christ the firstfruits; afterward they that are Christ's at his coming.""

Hebrews 9:12 Neither by the blood of goats and calves, but by his own blood he entered in once into the holy place, having obtained eternal redemption for us.

Hebrews 9:13 For if the blood of bulls and of goats, and the ashes of an heifer sprinkling the unclean, sanctifieth to the purifying of the flesh: 14 How much more shall the blood of Christ, who through the eternal Spirit offered himself without spot to God, purge your conscience from dead works to serve the living God? (KJV)

1 John 1:7 But if we walk in the light, as he is in the light, we have fellowship one with another, and the blood of Jesus Christ his Son cleanseth us from all sin. (KJV) 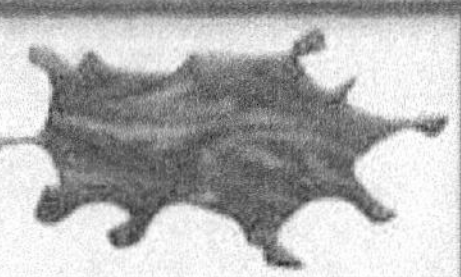

Here are some final Bible clues about hell, Sheol, and Hades:

What Bible verses describe hell?

Matthew 25:41 Then shall he say also unto them on the left hand, Depart from me, ye cursed, into everlasting fire, prepared for the devil and his angels. (KJV)

Matthew 10:28 And fear not them which kill the body, but are not able to kill the soul: but rather fear him which is able to destroy both soul and body in hell. (KJV)

Mark 9:43 And if thy hand offend thee, cut it off: it is better for thee to enter into life maimed, than having two hands to go into hell, into the fire that never shall be quenched. (KJV)

"We can know from what Jesus said that hell is an eternal (Matthew 25:41), physical (Matthew 10:28), and horrifying (Mark 9:43) place where those who've sinned (Romans 3:23) are headed, and from where Jesus Christ came to rescue all who would believe in him (John 3:16-18)."

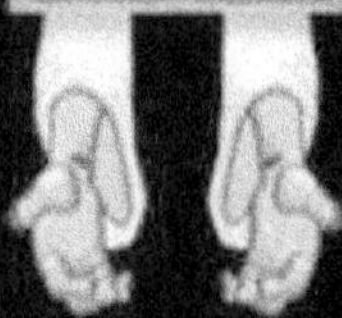

Romans 3:23 For all have sinned, and come short of the glory of God. (KJV)

John 3:16 For God so loved the world, that he gave his only begotten Son, that whosoever believeth in him should not perish, but have everlasting life.

John 3:17 For God sent not his Son into the world to condemn the world; but that the world through him might be saved.

John 3:18 He that believeth on him is not condemned: but he that believeth not is condemned already, because he hath not believed in the name of the only begotten Son of God. (KJV)

Let's try a thought experiment on what happened with Jesus' spirit between His crucifixion and resurrection. In trying to imagine what happened to all the sins Jesus absorbed from us on the Cross, let's explore one possible scenario that might have occurred.

Let's imagine one of the people who died in the flood that drowned all but Noah and his family of eight. Let's call him Teran in honor of Abraham's father. We know that Abraham's father, grandfather, and perhaps younger brother worshipped idols. Our imaginary Teran did as well. After dying, all idol worshippers were sent to the bad part of Hades for that sin against God.

So, when Jesus died on the Cross so that His Father could forgive our sins, Teran would also have been forgiven. So, would that mean he would suddenly be transferred from the bad side of Hades, the part where the rich man resided, to the good side of Hades, known as Abraham's bosom? It would be a bit like the two thieves who hung on the crosses on either side of our Lord. The thief on His left likely pictured continuing his life of sin if the Romans decided to release him. The thief on His right, who Jesus promised would be with Him in Paradise (i.e., Abraham's Bosom), likely pictured himself doing his best to live a sinless life. In the same way, it would depend on our imaginary Teran repenting of his sins and longing to live a life that would be pleasing to God.

So, perhaps Jesus first went to the Lake of Fire and dumped that immense load of sins so that we can be permanently separated from them, as long as we do our best not to keep repeatedly sinning. Next, Jesus might have gone to Abraham's Bosom to triumphantly lead Abraham, Adam and Eve, Abel, King David, the Prophets, and others who did their best to live God-pleasing lives to the Third Heaven, where our Father God resides. Then, He might have stood on the good side of Hades to gaze probingly and longingly at all His lost sheep residing in deep Hades. Jesus knew that anyone who truly belonged to Him would recognize His voice. Teran might have been in that select group.

An Angel of the Lord or the Holy Spirit might have shared the seven steps each man or woman would have to take to make a bridge appear so they could safely cross from one side of the abyss to the other. What were those steps?

1. Jesus, I accept you as my Savior.

2. Jesus, I accept you as my Lord and my King.

3. Jesus, I confess I sinned. This is what I did when I erred against you.

4. Jesus, I am so very sorry that I did those sins.

5. Jesus, please forgive me for those sins. I will not do them again.

6. Jesus, I forgive everyone who sinned against me, big sins or small.

7. Jesus, I want to follow you forever.

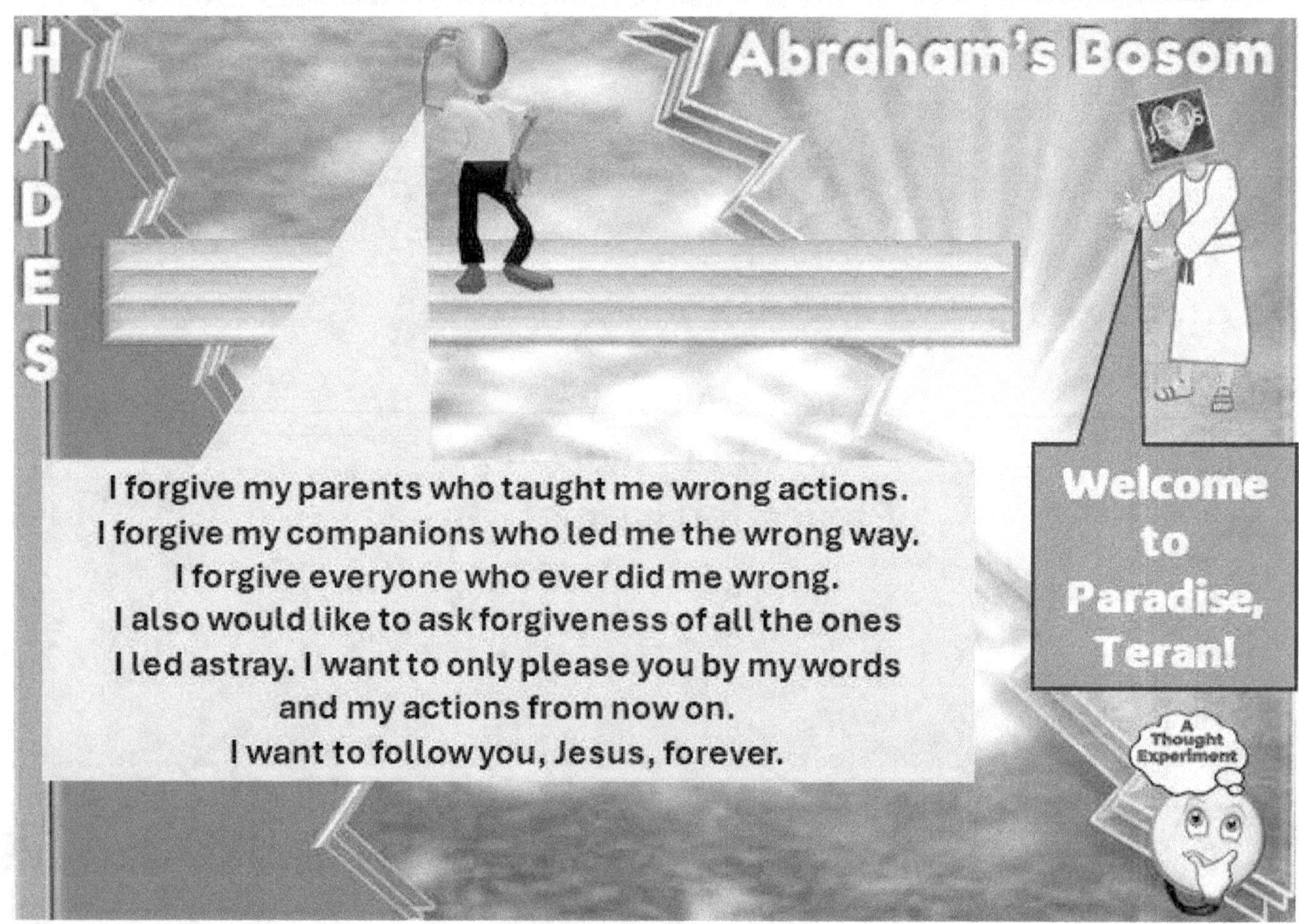

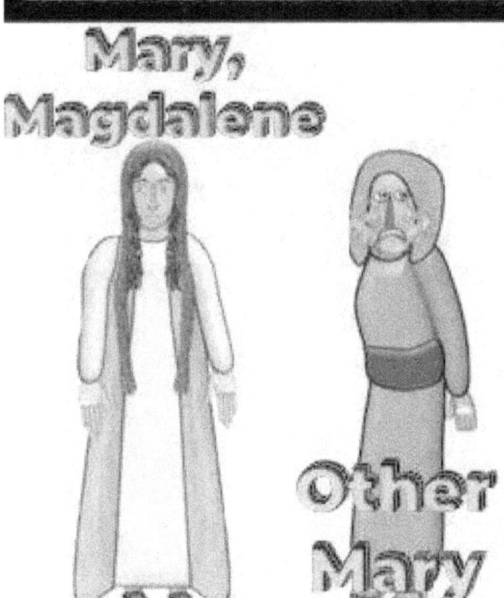

It's been parts of three days that Jesus' body lay in the tomb. Joseph of Arimathea and Nicodemus placed Him in the tomb between 3 PM and 6 PM on Friday. Saturday was the Sabbath. Guards who worked for Pilate guarded the tomb to prevent the Disciples from breaking in and stealing away His body.

It is just before dawn on Sunday. Mary Magdalene and one or more other ladies came to finish getting Jesus ready for burial. They wondered how they would manage to roll that heavy stone away to get inside the tomb. But to their shock and dismay, someone had already rolled the stone back, and Jesus was nowhere to be found.

On the 3rd day, Jesus rose from the dead.

Examine 4 Gospels for Clues (KJV)  

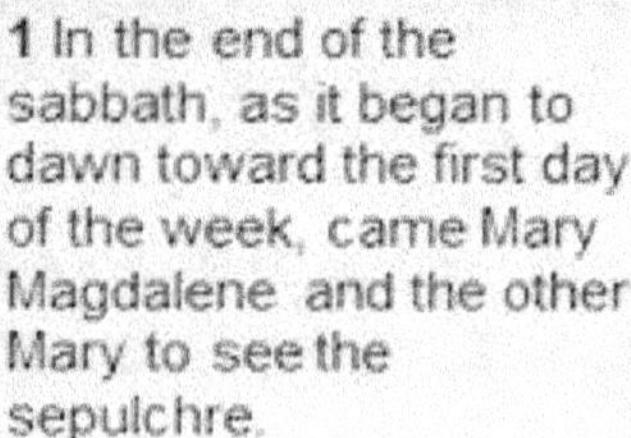

Matthew 28:1-4	Mark 16:1-4	Luke 24:1-3	John 20:1
1 In the end of the sabbath, as it began to dawn toward the first day of the week, came Mary Magdalene and the other Mary to see the sepulchre. **2** And, behold, there was a great earthquake: for the angel of the Lord descended from heaven, and came and rolled back the stone from the door, and sat upon it. **3** His countenance was like lightning, and his raiment white as snow: **4** And for fear of him the keepers did shake, and became as dead men.	**1** And when the sabbath was past, Mary Magdalene, and Mary the mother of James, and Salome, had bought sweet spices, that they might come and anoint him. **2** And very early in the morning the first day of the week, they came unto the sepulchre at the rising of the sun. **3** And they said among themselves, **Who shall roll us away the stone from the door of the sepulchre?** **4** And when they looked, they saw that the stone was rolled away: for it was very great.	**1** Now upon the first day of the week, very early in the morning, they came unto the sepulchre, bringing the spices which they had prepared, and certain others with them. **2** And they found the stone rolled away from the sepulchre. **3** And they entered in, and found not the body of the Lord Jesus.	**1** The first day of the week cometh Mary Magdalene early, when it was yet dark, unto the sepulchre, and seeth the stone taken away from the sepulchre. 

Examine 4 Gospels for Clues (KJV) 

Matthew 28:5-6	Mark 16:5-8	Luke 24:4-8	John 20:11-14
5 And the angel answered and said unto the women, **Fear not ye: for I know that ye seek Jesus, which was crucified.** **6 He is not here: for he is risen, as he said. Come, see the place where the Lord lay.**	**5** And entering into the sepulchre, they saw a young man sitting on the right side, clothed in a long white garment, and they were affrighted. **6** And he saith unto them, **Be not affrighted: Ye seek Jesus of Nazareth, which was crucified: he is risen; he is not here: behold the place where they laid him.** **7 But go your way, tell his disciples and Peter that he goeth before you into Galilee: there shall ye see him, as he said unto you.** **8** And they went out quickly, and fled from the sepulchre; for they trembled and were amazed: neither said they any thing to any man; for they were afraid.	**4** And it came to pass, as they were much perplexed thereabout, behold, two men stood by them in shining garments: **5** And as they were afraid, and bowed down their faces to the earth, they said unto them, **Why seek ye the living among the dead?** **6 He is not here, but is risen: remember how he spake unto you when he was yet in Galilee, 7 Saying, The Son of man must be delivered into the hands of sinful men, and be crucified, and the third day rise again.** **8** And they remembered his words.	**11** But Mary stood without at the sepulchre weeping: and as she wept, she stooped down, and looked into the sepulchre, **12** And seeth two angels in white sitting, the one at the head, and the other at the feet, where the body of Jesus had lain. **13** And they say unto her, **Woman, why weepest thou?** She saith unto them, **Because they have taken away my Lord, and I know not where they have laid him.** **14** And when she had thus said, she turned herself back, and saw Jesus standing, and knew not that it was Jesus.

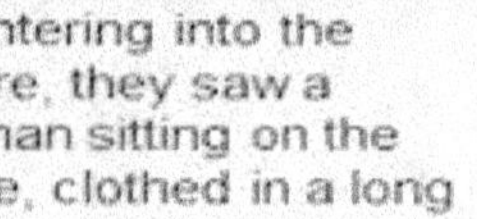
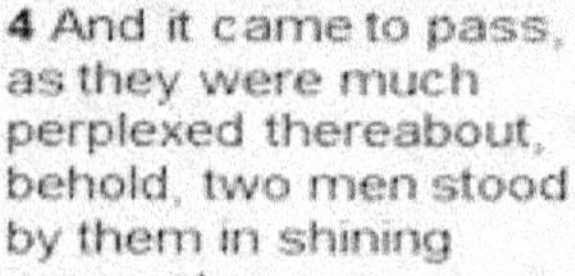

CONTINUED

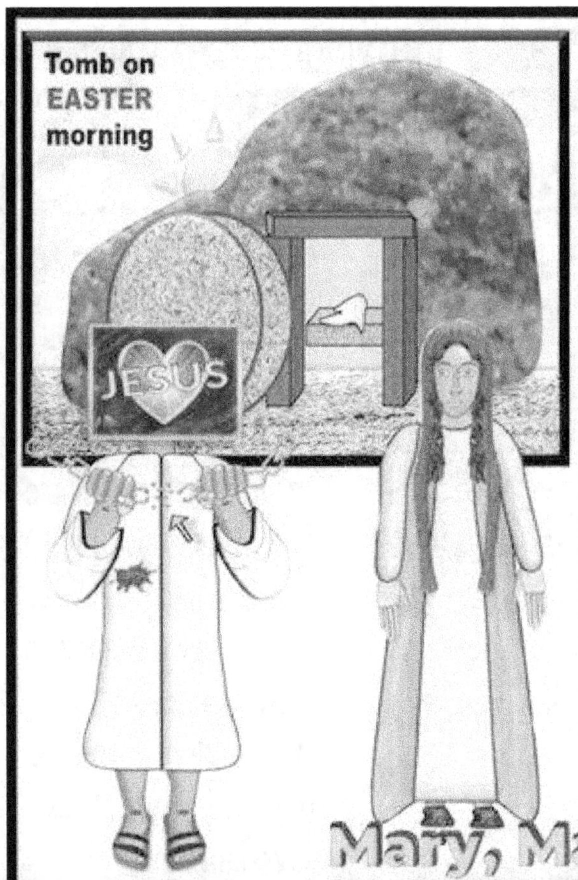

John 20:15 Jesus saith unto her, Woman, why weepest thou? whom seekest thou? She, supposing him to be the gardener, saith unto him, Sir, if thou have borne him hence, tell me where thou hast laid him, and I will take him away.

John 20:16 Jesus saith unto her, Mary. She turned herself, and saith unto him, Rabboni; which is to say, Master.

John 20:17 Jesus saith unto her, Touch me not; for I am not yet ascended to my Father: but go to my brethren, and say unto them, I ascend unto my Father, and your Father; and to my God, and your God.

John 20:18 Mary Magdalene came and told the disciples that she had seen the Lord, and that he had spoken these things unto her.

On the 3rd day, Jesus rose from the dead.

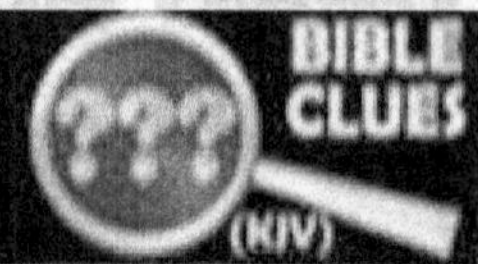

Examine 4 Gospels for Clues (KJV)

 **Matthew** 28:7-10    **Mark** 16:9-11    **Luke** 24:9-12    **John** 20:2-5

Matthew 28:7-10

7 And go quickly, and tell his disciples that he is risen from the dead; and, behold, he goeth before you into Galilee; there shall ye see him: lo, I have told you.

8 And they departed quickly from the sepulchre with fear and great joy; and did run to bring his disciples word.

9 And as they [Mary Magdalene and the other Mary] went to tell his disciples, behold, Jesus met them, saying, **All hail.** And they came and held him by the feet, and worshipped him.

10 Then said Jesus unto them, **Be not afraid: go tell my brethren that they go into Galilee, and there shall they see me.**

Mark 16:9-11

9 Now when Jesus was risen early the first day of the week, he appeared first to Mary Magdalene, out of whom he had cast seven devils.

10 And she went and told them that had been with him, as they mourned and wept.

11 And they, when they had heard that he was alive, and had been seen of her, believed not.

Luke 24:9-12

9 And returned from the sepulchre, and told all these things unto the eleven, and to all the rest.

10 It was Mary Magdalene and Joanna, and Mary the mother of James, and other women that were with them, which told these things unto the apostles.

11 And their words seemed to them as idle tales, and they believed them not.

12 Then arose Peter, and ran unto the sepulchre; and stooping down, he beheld the linen clothes laid by themselves, and departed, wondering in himself at that which was come to pass.

John 20:2-5

2 Then she runneth, and cometh to Simon Peter, and to the other disciple, whom Jesus loved [i.e., John Z.], and saith unto them, **They have taken away the Lord out of the sepulchre, and we know not where they have laid him.**

3 Peter therefore went forth, and that other disciple, and came to the sepulchre.

4 So they ran both together: and the other disciple [i.e., John Z.] did outrun Peter, and came first to the sepulchre.

5 And he stooping down, and looking in, saw the linen clothes lying; yet went he not in.

CONTINUED 

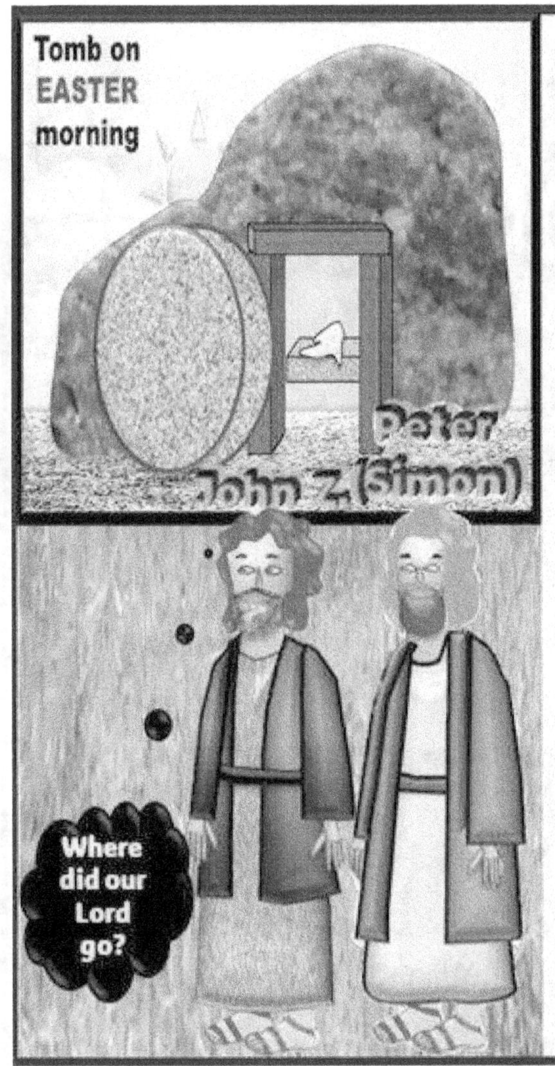

John 20:6 Then cometh Simon Peter following him, and went into the sepulchre, and seeth the linen clothes lie, 7 And the napkin, that was about his head, not lying with the linen clothes, but wrapped together in a place by itself.

John 20:8 Then went in also that other disciple [i.e., John Z.], which came first to the sepulchre, and he saw, and believed.

John 20:9 For as yet they knew not the scripture, that he must rise again from the dead.

John 20:10 Then the disciples went away again unto their own home. (KJV)

The risen Jesus met with two men on the road.

Examine 4 Gospels for Clues (KJV)

Mark 16:12-13

Luke 24:13-24

12 After that he appeared in another form unto two of them, as they walked, and went into the country.

13 And they went and told it unto the residue: neither believed they them.

13 And, behold, two of them went that same day to a village called Emmaus, which was from Jerusalem about threescore furlongs. **14** And they talked together of all these things which had happened. **15** And it came to pass, that, while they communed together and reasoned, Jesus himself drew near, and went with them. **16** But their eyes were holden that they should not know him.

17 And he said unto them, **What manner of communications are these that ye have one to another, as ye walk, and are sad?**

18 And the one of them, whose name was Cleopas, answering said unto him, **Art thou only a stranger in Jerusalem, and hast not known the things which are come to pass there in these days?**

19 And he said unto them, **What things?** And they said unto him, **Concerning Jesus of Nazareth, which was a prophet mighty in deed and word before God and all the people: 20 And how the chief priests and our rulers delivered him to be condemned to death, and have crucified him.**

21 But we trusted that it had been he which should have redeemed Israel: and beside all this, to day is the third day since these things were done.

22 Yea, and certain women also of our company made us astonished, which were early at the sepulchre; **23** And when they found not his body, they came, saying, that they had also seen a vision of angels, which said that he was alive. **24** And certain of them which were with us went to the sepulchre, and found it even so as the women had said: but him they saw not.

Luke 24:25 Then he said unto them, O fools, and slow of heart to believe all that the prophets have spoken: 26 Ought not Christ to have suffered these things, and to enter into his glory?

Luke 24:27 And beginning at Moses and all the prophets, he expounded unto them in all the scriptures the things concerning himself.

Luke 24:28 And they drew nigh unto the village, whither they went: and he made as though he would have gone further. 29 But they constrained him, saying, Abide with us: for it is toward evening, and the day is far spent. **And he went in to tarry with them.**

Luke 24:30 And it came to pass, as he sat at meat with them, he took bread, and blessed it, and brake, and gave to them. **31 And their eyes were opened, and they knew him; and he vanished out of their sight.**

Luke 24:32 And they said one to another, Did not our heart burn within us, while he talked with us by the way, and while he opened to us the scriptures?

Luke 24:33 And they [i.e., Cleopas and another man] rose up the same hour, and returned to Jerusalem, and found the eleven gathered together, and them that were with them, 34 Saying, The Lord is risen indeed, and hath appeared to Simon.

??? WHICH SIMON ARE THEY REFERENCING ???

Luke 24:35 And they told what things were done in the way, and how he was known of them in breaking of bread.

Luke 24:36 And as they thus spake, Jesus himself stood in the midst of them, and saith unto them, Peace be unto you.

Luke 24:37 But they were terrified and affrighted, and supposed that they had seen a spirit. (KJV)

Pharisees deny that Christ Jesus was resurrected.

Examine 4 Gospels for Clues (KJV)

Matthew 28:11-15
TRICK PLAYED BY THE PHARISEES

11 Now when they were going, behold, some of the watch came into the city, and shewed unto the chief priests all the things that were done.

12 And when they were assembled with the elders, and had taken counsel, they gave large money unto the soldiers,

13 Saying, Say ye, His disciples came by night, and stole him away while we slept. **14** And if this come to the governor's ears, we will persuade him, and secure you.

15 So they took the money, and did as they were taught: and this saying is commonly reported among the Jews until this day.

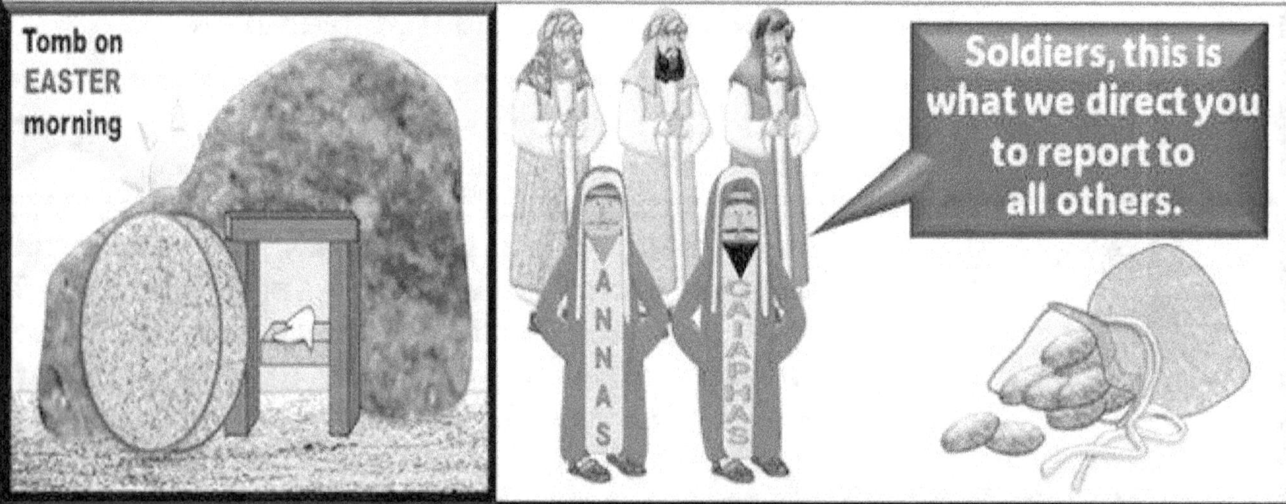

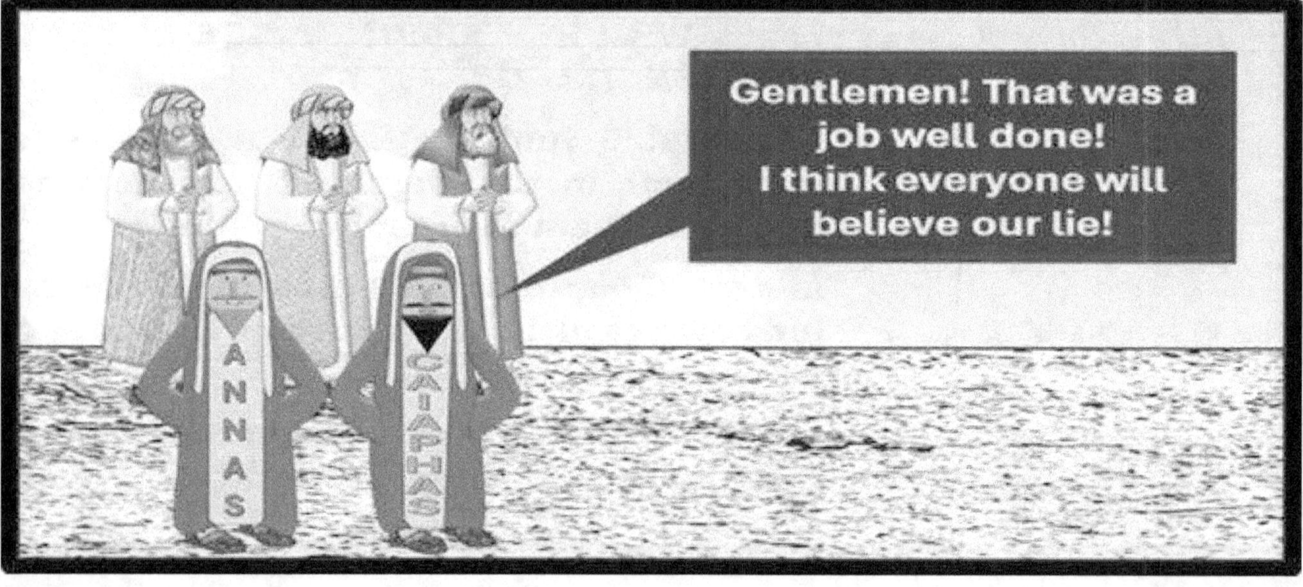

The risen Jesus met with 10 of the 11 Disciples.

Examine 4 Gospels for Clues (KJV)

Matthew 28:16-17	Mark 16:14	Luke 24:38-43	John 20:19-23
16 Then the eleven disciples went away into Galilee, into a mountain where Jesus had appointed them. **17** And when they saw him, they worshipped him: but some doubted.	**14** Afterward he appeared unto the eleven as they sat at meat, and upbraided them with their unbelief and hardness of heart, because they believed not them which had seen him after he was risen.	**38** And he said unto them, Why are ye troubled? and why do thoughts arise in your hearts? **39** Behold my hands and my feet, that it is I myself: handle me, and see; for a spirit hath not flesh and bones, as ye see me have. **40** And when he had thus spoken, he shewed them his hands and his feet. **41** And while they yet believed not for joy, and wondered, he said unto them, Have ye here any meat? **42** And they gave him a piece of a broiled fish, and of an honeycomb. **43** And he took it, and did eat before them.	**19** Then the same day at evening, being the first day of the week, when the doors were shut where the disciples were assembled for fear of the Jews, came Jesus and stood in the midst, and saith unto them, Peace be unto you. **20** And when he had so said, he shewed unto them his hands and his side. Then were the disciples glad, when they saw the Lord. **21** Then said Jesus to them again, Peace be unto you: as my Father hath sent me, even so send I you. **22** And when he had said this, he breathed on them, and saith unto them, Receive ye the Holy Ghost: **23** Whose soever sins ye remit, they are remitted unto them; and whose soever sins ye retain, they are retained.

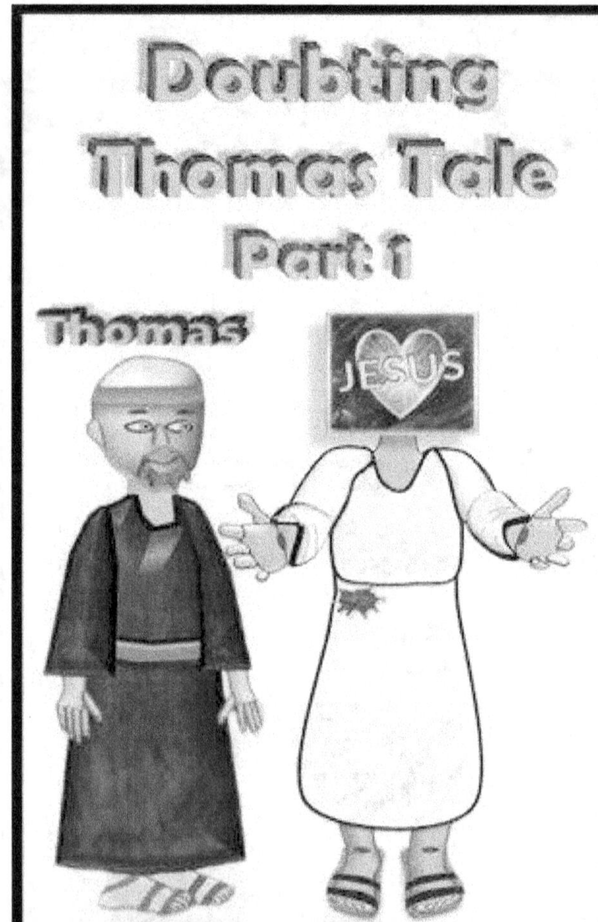

John 20:24 But Thomas, one of the twelve, called Didymus, was not with them when Jesus came.

John 20:25 The other disciples therefore said unto him, We have seen the Lord. But he said unto them, Except I shall see in his hands the print of the nails, and put my finger into the print of the nails, and thrust my hand into his side, I will not believe.

John 20:26 And after eight days again his disciples were within, and Thomas with them: then came Jesus, the doors being shut, and stood in the midst, and said, Peace be unto you.

John 20:27 Then saith he to Thomas, Reach hither thy finger, and behold my hands; and reach hither thy hand, and thrust it into my side: and be not faithless, but believing.

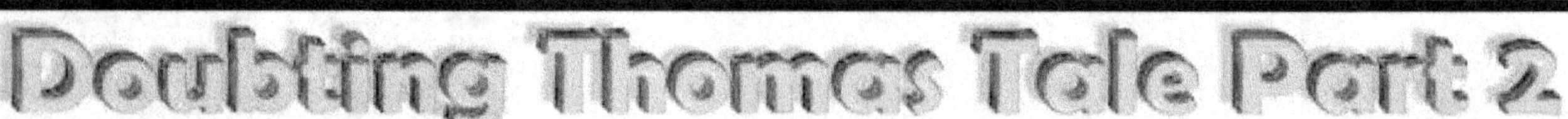

John 20:28 And Thomas answered and said unto him, My Lord and my God.

John 20:29 Jesus saith unto him, Thomas, because thou hast seen me, thou hast believed: blessed are they that have not seen, and yet have believed.

John 20:30 And many other signs truly did Jesus in the presence of his disciples, which are not written in this book:

John 20:31 But these are written, that ye might believe that Jesus is the Christ, the Son of God; and that believing ye might have life through his name.

Examine 4 Gospels for Clues (KJV)

John 21:1-14

1 After these things Jesus shewed himself again to the disciples at the sea of Tiberias; and on this wise shewed he himself.

2 There were together Simon Peter, and Thomas called Didymus, and Nathanael of Cana in Galilee, and the sons of Zebedee, and two other of his disciples. 3 Simon Peter saith unto them, **I go a fishing.** They say unto him, **We also go with thee.** They went forth, and entered into a ship immediately; and that night they caught nothing.

4 But when the morning was now come, Jesus stood on the shore: but the disciples knew not that it was Jesus. 5 Then Jesus saith unto them, **Children, have ye any meat?** They answered him, **No.**

6 And he said unto them, **Cast the net on the right side of the ship, and ye shall find.** They cast therefore, and now they were not able to draw it for the multitude of fishes.

7 Therefore that disciple whom Jesus loved [i.e., John Z.] saith unto Peter, **It is the Lord.** Now when Simon Peter heard that it was the Lord, he girt his fisher's coat unto him, (for he was naked,) and did cast himself into the sea.

8 And the other disciples came in a little ship; (for they were not far from land, but as it were two hundred cubits,) dragging the net with fishes.

9 As soon then as they were come to land, they saw a fire of coals there, and fish laid thereon, and bread.

10 Jesus saith unto them, **Bring of the fish which ye have now caught.**

11 Simon Peter went up, and drew the net to land full of great fishes, an hundred and fifty and three: and for all there were so many, yet was not the net broken.

12 Jesus saith unto them, **Come and dine.** And none of the disciples durst ask him, **Who art thou?** knowing that it was the Lord.

13 Jesus then cometh, and taketh bread, and giveth them, and fish likewise.

14 This is now the third time that Jesus shewed himself to his disciples, after that he was risen from the dead.

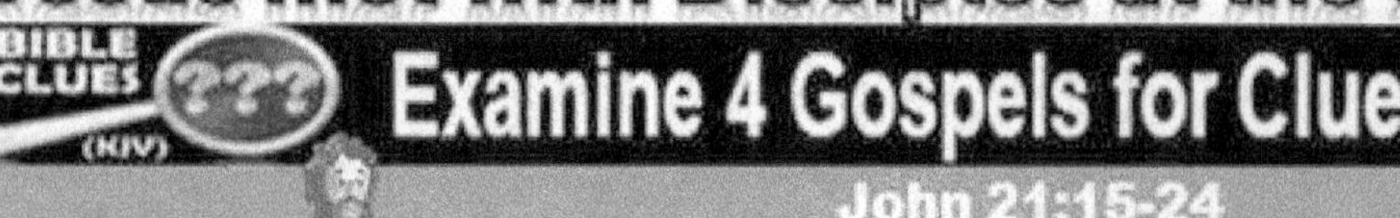

Examine 4 Gospels for Clues (KJV)

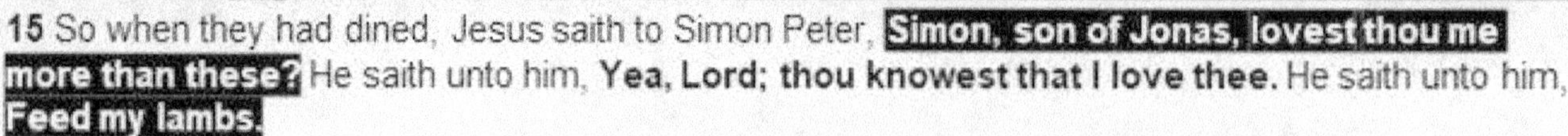

John 21:15-24

15 So when they had dined, Jesus saith to Simon Peter, **Simon, son of Jonas, lovest thou me more than these?** He saith unto him, **Yea, Lord; thou knowest that I love thee.** He saith unto him, **Feed my lambs.**

16 He saith to him again the second time, **Simon, son of Jonas, lovest thou me?** He saith unto him, **Yea, Lord; thou knowest that I love thee.** He saith unto him, **Feed my sheep.**

17 He saith unto him the third time, **Simon, son of Jonas, lovest thou me?** Peter was grieved because he said unto him the third time, **Lovest thou me?** And he said unto him, **Lord, thou knowest all things; thou knowest that I love thee.** Jesus saith unto him, **Feed my sheep.**

18 **Verily, verily, I say unto thee, When thou wast young, thou girdest thyself, and walkedst whither thou wouldest: but when thou shalt be old, thou shalt stretch forth thy hands, and another shall gird thee, and carry thee whither thou wouldest not.**

19 This spake he, signifying by what death he should glorify God. And when he had spoken this, he saith unto him, **Follow me.**

20 Then Peter, turning about, seeth the disciple whom Jesus loved [i.e., John Z.] following; which also leaned on his breast at supper, and said, **Lord, which is he that betrayeth thee?**

21 Peter seeing him saith to Jesus, **Lord, and what shall this man do?**

22 Jesus saith unto him, **If I will that he tarry till I come, what is that to thee? follow thou me.**

23 Then went this saying abroad among the brethren, that that disciple should not die: yet Jesus said not unto him, **He shall not die; but, If I will that he tarry till I come, what is that to thee?**

24 This is the disciple [i.e., John Z.] which testifieth of these things, and wrote these things: and we know that his testimony is true.

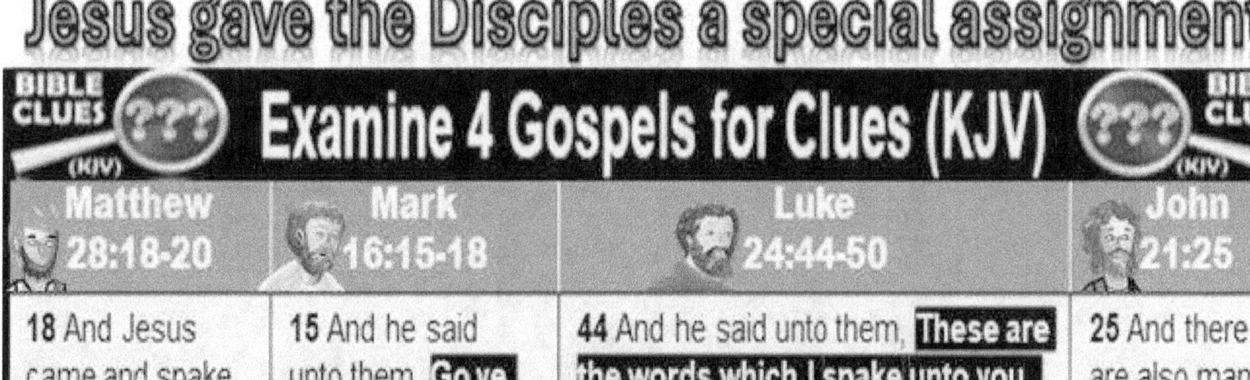

Matthew 28:18-20	Mark 16:15-18	Luke 24:44-50	John 21:25
18 And Jesus came and spake unto them, saying, All power is given unto me in heaven and in earth. **19** Go ye therefore, and teach all nations, baptizing them in the name of the Father, and of the Son, and of the Holy Ghost: **20** Teaching them to observe all things whatsoever I have commanded you: and, lo, I am with you always, even unto the end of the world. Amen.	**15** And he said unto them, Go ye into all the world, and preach the gospel to every creature. **16** He that believeth and is baptized shall be saved; but he that believeth not shall be damned. **17** And these signs shall follow them that believe; In my name shall they cast out devils; they shall speak with new tongues; **18** They shall take up serpents; and if they drink any deadly thing, it shall not hurt them; they shall lay hands on the sick, and they shall recover.	**44** And he said unto them, These are the words which I spake unto you, while I was yet with you, that all things must be fulfilled, which were written in the law of Moses, and in the prophets, and in the psalms, concerning me. **45** Then opened he their understanding, that they might understand the scriptures, **46** And said unto them, Thus it is written, and thus it behooved Christ to suffer, and to rise from the dead the third day: **47** And that repentance and remission of sins should be preached in his name among all nations, beginning at Jerusalem. **48** And ye are witnesses of these things. **49** And, behold, I send the promise of my Father upon you: but tarry ye in the city of Jerusalem, until ye be endued with power from on high. **50** And he led them out as far as to Bethany, and he lifted up his hands, and blessed them.	**25** And there are also many other things which Jesus did, the which, if they should be written every one, I suppose that even the world itself could not contain the books that should be written. Amen.

Our Lord Jesus ascended into Heaven. Amen.

BIBLE CLUES (KJV) — Examine 4 Gospels for Clues (KJV) — BIBLE CLUES (KJV)

Mark 16:19-20

19 So then after the Lord had spoken unto them, he was received up into heaven, and sat on the right hand of God.

20 And they went forth, and preached every where, the Lord working with them, and confirming the word with signs following. Amen.

Luke 24:51-53

51 And it came to pass, while he blessed them, he was parted from them, and carried up into heaven.

52 And they worshipped him, and returned to Jerusalem with great joy: **53** And were continually in the temple, praising and blessing God. Amen.

1. What do we know about Joseph of Arimathea?

2. Describe what happened at the Tomb on Friday.

3. What is your theory about why many of the Jewish people did not believe Jesus was the true Messiah?

4. Discuss the Remez Old Testament statements mentioned in the last few chapters. Which ones impacted you the most and why?

5. What is your theory of what happened to Jesus in the time period between the Crucifixion and His Resurrection?

6. Describe what happened to Jonah. How does that compare to what happened to Jesus?

7. There is a lot of controversy about the exact years Jesus was born and died. The author chose to side with the Biblical scholars that stated He was born in 4 BC and died in 30 AD. Do you have a similar or different theory? Please explain your answer.

8. What kind of things do you think were going through the minds of the Disciples, Jesus' mother, and Mary Magdalene on Saturday, His second day in the tomb?

9. Explain your theory of how Jesus managed to atone for over 100 trillion sins.

10. Describe what happened between Jesus and Mary Magdalene on Sunday.

11. Describe what happened between Jesus and the Disciples.

12. Describe what happened between Jesus and the two men on the road.

13. Describe the trick that was played by the Pharisees when they discovered that the tomb was empty.

14. What was the special assignment Jesus given to the 11 Disciples?

40 DAYS SPENT WITH THE RISEN JESUS CHRIST

Can you imagine how awe-inspiring it would have been to spend 40 days with your teacher, whom God had resurrected? You likely would have been full of questions to which He alone would have been qualified to answer.

At the end of the forty days, you would have witnessed the unique view of Jesus ascending into Heaven. As you stared in amazement, two angels spoke to you, asking why you continued looking upward when He was gone from view.

Lastly, Jesus cautioned you to remain in Jerusalem so that you could experience the baptism of the Holy Ghost, also known as the Holy Spirit. That would indeed have been a spectacular experience!

Acts 1:1 The former treatise have I made, O Theophilus, of all that Jesus began both to do and teach, 2 Until the day in which he was taken up, after that he through the Holy Ghost had given commandments unto the apostles whom he had chosen: 3 To whom also he shewed himself alive after his passion by many infallible proofs, being seen of them forty days, and speaking of the things pertaining to the kingdom of God: 4 And, being assembled together with them, commanded them that they should not depart from Jerusalem, but wait for the promise of the Father, which, saith he, ye have heard of me. (KJV)

Acts 1: 5 to 6

Jesus spent 40 days with them.

Acts 1:5 For John truly baptized with water; but ye shall be baptized with the Holy Ghost not many days hence.

Acts 1:6 When they therefore were come together, they asked of him, saying, Lord, wilt thou at this time restore again the kingdom to Israel? (KJV)

Acts 1: 7 to 8

Jesus spent 40 days with them.

Acts 1:7 And he said unto them, It is not for you to know the times or the seasons, which the Father hath put in his own power.

Acts 1:8 But ye shall receive power, after that the Holy Ghost is come upon you: and ye shall be witnesses unto me both in Jerusalem, and in all Judaea, and in Samaria, and unto the uttermost part of the earth. (KJV)

Acts 1: 9

Jesus spent 40 days with them.

Acts 1:9 And when he had spoken these things, while they beheld, he was taken up; and a cloud received him out of their sight.

Acts 1: 10 to 11

Jesus spent 40 days with them.

Acts 1:10 And while they looked stedfastly toward heaven as he went up, behold, two men stood by them in white apparel; 11 Which also said, Ye men of Galilee, why stand ye gazing up into heaven? this same Jesus, which is taken up from you into heaven, shall so come in like manner as ye have seen him go into heaven. (KJV)

The Book of Acts: Description and Author

Describe the Book of Acts

"The Book of Acts is mainly about the introduction to the Holy Spirit and the enabling power of the Spirit in the lives of believers. Though many people are introduced throughout the book, the primary protagonists are the Apostle Peter (Chapters 3-12) and the Apostle Paul (Chapters 9-28)."

"Acts and the Gospel of Luke make up a two-part work, Luke–Acts, by the same anonymous author. Traditionally, the author is believed to be Luke the Evangelist, a doctor who travelled with Paul the Apostle. It is usually dated to around 80–90 AD, although some scholars suggest 110–120 AD."

Book of Acts

CHOOSING A REPLACEMENT FOR JUDAS

In the first part of **Acts 1**, we learn that Jesus spent the first 40 days of His resurrection instructing His Disciples. Before ascending on the 40th day, He instructed His closest followers to wait in Jerusalem for the visitation of the Holy Spirit.

In **Acts 1:12-13**, we learn that the eleven remaining Disciples walked from the Mount of Olives to the room in Jerusalem where they were staying. This group included:

1. **Peter, also known as Simon Peter**
2. **John Z., brother of James**
3. **James Z., brother of John**
4. **Andrew, brother of Peter**
5. **Philip**
6. **Thomas**
7. **Bartholomew, also known as Nathanael or Nathaniel**
8. **Matthew, a former Tax Collector**
9. **Little James, son of Alphaeus**
10. **Simon the Zealot**
11. **Judas, son of James, also known as Thaddaeus or Jude**

Pentecost would not happen for ten more days.

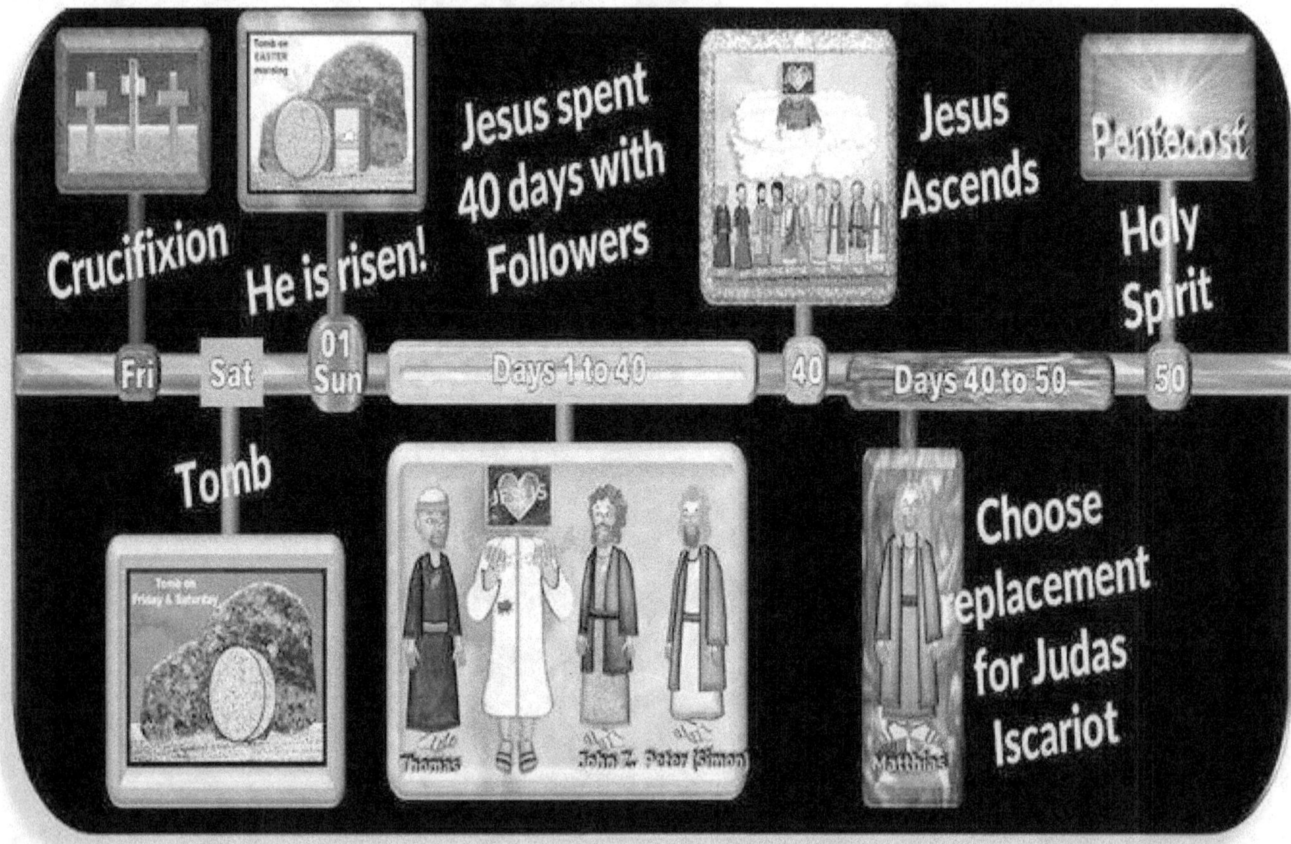

 **In Acts 1:14**, we learn that the Disciples, the women followers, and the brothers and mother of Jesus spent their waiting time in prayer.

As Peter contemplated the betrayal and subsequent suicide of Judas Iscariot, he must have felt inspired after reading these verses in Psalm and Proverbs.

Psalm 69:25 May their place be deserted; let there be no one to dwell in their tents.

Psalm 109:8 May his days be few; may another take his place of leadership.

Proverbs 16:33 The lot is cast into the lap, but its every decision is from the Lord.

One night, Peter stood up and announced the following:

Acts 1:15 In those days Peter stood up among the believers (a group numbering about a hundred and twenty)

Acts 1:16 and said, "Brothers and sisters, the Scripture had to be fulfilled in which the Holy Spirit spoke long ago through David concerning Judas, who served as guide for those who arrested Jesus.

Acts 1:17 He was one of our number and shared in our ministry."

Acts 1:18 (With the payment he received for his wickedness, Judas bought a field; there he fell headlong, his body burst open and all his intestines spilled out.

Acts 1:19 Everyone in Jerusalem heard about this, so they called that field in their language Akeldama, that is, Field of Blood.)

Acts 1:20 "For," said Peter, "it is written in the Book of Psalm: 'May his place be deserted; let there be no one to dwell in it,' and, 'May another take his place of leadership.'

Acts 1:21 Therefore it is necessary to choose one of the men who have been with us the whole time the Lord Jesus was living among us, 22 beginning from John's baptism to the time when Jesus was taken up from us. For one of these must become a witness with us of his resurrection."

Acts 1:23 So they nominated two men: Joseph called Barsabbas (also known as Justus) and Matthias.

Acts 1:24 Then they prayed, "Lord, you know everyone's heart. Show us which of these two you have chosen **25** to take over this apostolic ministry, which Judas left to go where he belongs."

Acts 1:26 Then they cast lots, and the lot fell to Matthias; so he was added to the eleven apostles.

Acts 1: 12 to 26

There is no other mention of Matthias' name in the Bible.

What happened to Matthias?

As you can see from the quote below, Matthias preached the Gospel in Judea (modern day Israel) and Colchis (western part of Georgia).

He was crucified in 80 AD.

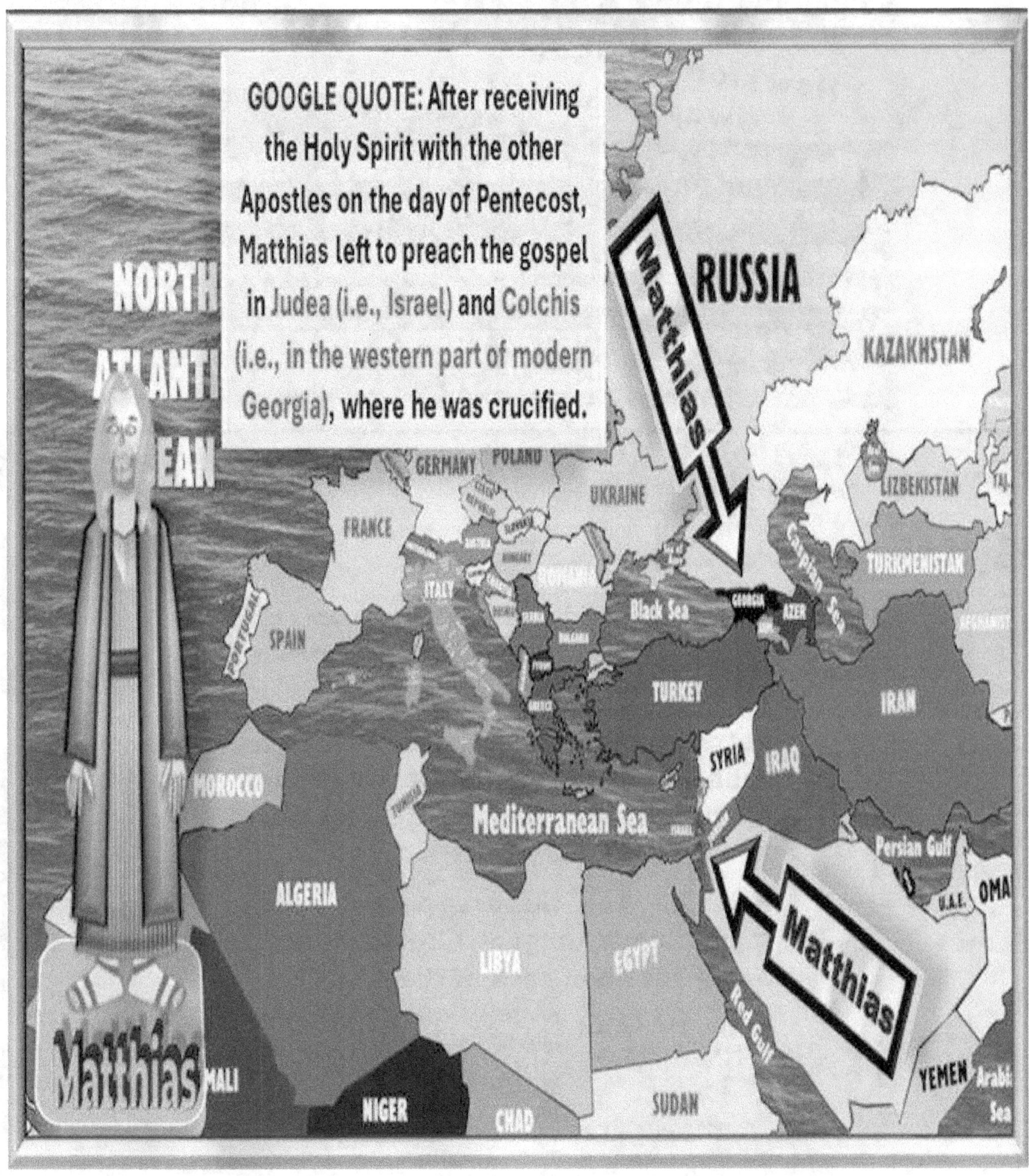

PENTECOST AND THE HOLY SPIRIT

The Bible verses in this chapter describes what happened at Pentecost.

How many days after the resurrection was the day of Pentecost?

"The Holy Spirit came 50 days after the resurrection, 10 days after the ascension. Jews of many nations had gathered in Jerusalem to celebrate the festival. When the day of Pentecost came, they were all together in one place."

Acts 2: 1 to 4
PENTECOST

Acts 2:1 And when the day of Pentecost was fully come, they were all with one accord in one place.

Acts 2:2 And suddenly there came a sound from heaven as of a rushing mighty wind, and it filled all the house where they were sitting.

Acts 2:3 And there appeared unto them cloven tongues like as of fire, and it sat upon each of them.

Acts 2:4 And they were all filled with the Holy Ghost, and began to speak with other tongues, as the Spirit gave them utterance. (KJV)

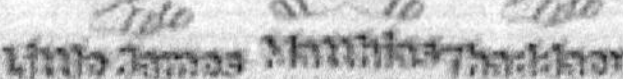

Acts 2: 5 to 8 — PENTECOST

Acts 2:5 And there were dwelling at Jerusalem Jews, devout men, out of every nation under heaven.

Acts 2:6 Now when this was noised abroad, the multitude came together, and were confounded, because that every man heard them speak in his own language.

Acts 2:7 And they were all amazed and marvelled, saying one to another, Behold, are not all these which speak Galilaeans?

Acts 2:8 And how hear we every man in our own tongue, wherein we were born? (KJV)

Acts 2: 9 to 13 — PENTECOST

Acts 2:9 Parthians, and Medes, and Elamites, and the dwellers in Mesopotamia, and in Judaea, and Cappadocia, in Pontus, and Asia, 10 Phrygia, and Pamphylia, in Egypt, and in the parts of Libya about Cyrene, and strangers of Rome, Jews and proselytes, 11 Cretes and Arabians, we do hear them speak in our tongues the wonderful works of God.

Acts 2:12 And they were all amazed, and were in doubt, saying one to another, What meaneth this? (KJV)

Acts 2:13 Others mocking said, These men are full of new wine.

Acts 2: 14 to 18 — PENTECOST

Acts 2:14 But Peter, standing up with the eleven, lifted up his voice, and said unto them, Ye men of Judaea, and all ye that dwell at Jerusalem, be this known unto you, and hearken to my words: 15 For these are not drunken, as ye suppose, seeing it is but the third hour of the day [i.e., 9 AM].

Acts 2:16 But this is that which was spoken by the prophet Joel; 17 And it shall come to pass in the last days, saith God, I will pour out of my Spirit upon all flesh: and your sons and your daughters shall prophesy, and your young men shall see visions, and your old men shall dream dreams: 18 And on my servants and on my handmaidens I will pour out in those days of my Spirit; and they shall prophesy: (KJV)

Acts 2: 19 to 24 — PENTECOST

Acts 2:19 And I will shew wonders in heaven above, and signs in the earth beneath; blood, and fire, and vapour of smoke: 20 The sun shall be turned into darkness, and the moon into blood, before the great and notable day of the Lord come: 21 And it shall come to pass, that whosoever shall call on the name of the Lord shall be saved.

Acts 2:22 Ye men of Israel, hear these words; Jesus of Nazareth, a man approved of God among you by miracles and wonders and signs, which God did by him in the midst of you, as ye yourselves also know: 23 Him, being delivered by the determinate counsel and foreknowledge of God, ye have taken, and by wicked hands have crucified and slain: 24 Whom God hath raised up, having loosed the pains of death: because it was not possible that he should be holden of it. (KJV)

Acts 2: 25 to 29 — PENTECOST

Acts 2:25 For David speaketh concerning him, I foresaw the Lord always before my face, for he is on my right hand, that I should not be moved: **26** Therefore did my heart rejoice, and my tongue was glad; moreover also my flesh shall rest in hope: **27** Because thou wilt not leave my soul in hell, neither wilt thou suffer thine Holy One to see corruption.

Acts 2:28 Thou hast made known to me the ways of life; thou shalt make me full of joy with thy countenance.

Acts 2:29 Men and brethren, let me freely speak unto you of the patriarch David, that he is both dead and buried, and his sepulchre is with us unto this day. **(KJV)**

Acts 2: 30 to 33 — PENTECOST

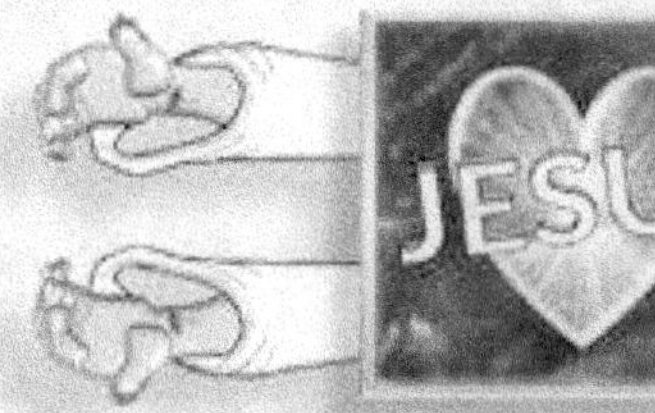

Acts 2:30 Therefore being a prophet, and knowing that God had sworn with an oath to him, that of the fruit of his loins, according to the flesh, he would raise up Christ to sit on his throne; **31** He seeing this before spake of the resurrection of Christ, that his soul was not left in hell, neither his flesh did see corruption. **God**

Acts 2:32 This Jesus hath God raised up, whereof we all are witnesses. **33** Therefore being by the right hand of God exalted, and having received of the Father the promise of the Holy Ghost, he hath shed forth this, which ye now see and hear. **(KJV)**

Acts 2: 34 to 37 — PENTECOST

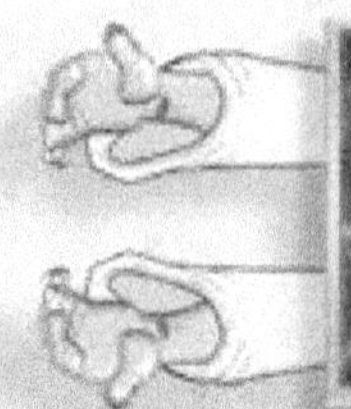

Acts 2:34 For David is not ascended into the heavens: but he saith himself, The Lord said unto my Lord, Sit thou on my right hand, 35 Until I make thy foes thy footstool.

Acts 2:36 Therefore let all the house of Israel know assuredly, that God hath made the same Jesus, whom ye have crucified, both Lord and Christ.

Acts 2:37 Now when they heard this, they were pricked in their heart, and said unto Peter and to the rest of the apostles, Men and brethren, what shall we do? (KJV)

Acts 2: 38 to 40 — PENTECOST

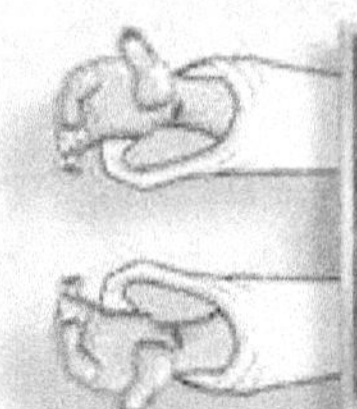

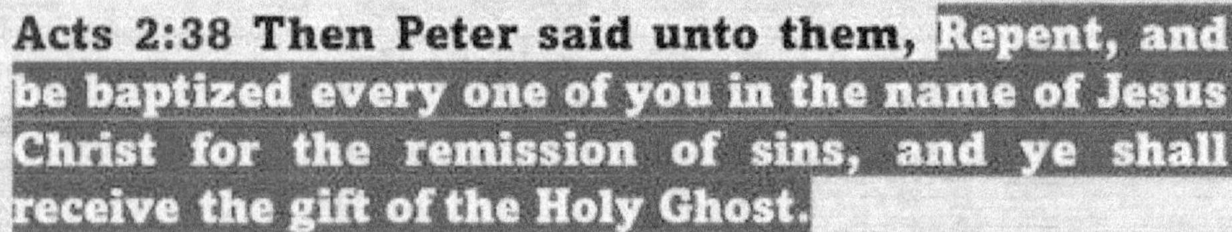

Acts 2:38 Then Peter said unto them, Repent, and be baptized every one of you in the name of Jesus Christ for the remission of sins, and ye shall receive the gift of the Holy Ghost.

Acts 2:39 For the promise is unto you, and to your children, and to all that are afar off, even as many as the Lord our God shall call.

Acts 2:40 And with many other words did he testify and exhort, saying, Save yourselves from this untoward generation. (KJV)

Acts 2: 41 to 43   PENTECOST

Acts 2:41 Then they that gladly received his word were baptized: and the same day there were added unto them about three thousand souls.

Acts 2:42 And they continued stedfastly in the apostles' doctrine and fellowship, and in breaking of bread, and in prayers.

Acts 2:43 And fear came upon every soul: and many wonders and signs were done by the apostles. (KJV)

Acts 2: 44 to 47   PENTECOST

Acts 2:44 And all that believed were together, and had all things common; 45 And sold their possessions and goods, and parted them to all men, as every man had need.

Acts 2:46 And they, continuing daily with one accord in the temple, and breaking bread from house to house, did eat their meat with gladness and singleness of heart, 47 Praising God, and having favour with all the people. And the Lord added to the church daily such as should be saved. (KJV)

MORE DETAILS ABOUT THE HOLY SPIRIT

This is list of attributes of the Holy Spirit as described by the Prophet Isaiah:

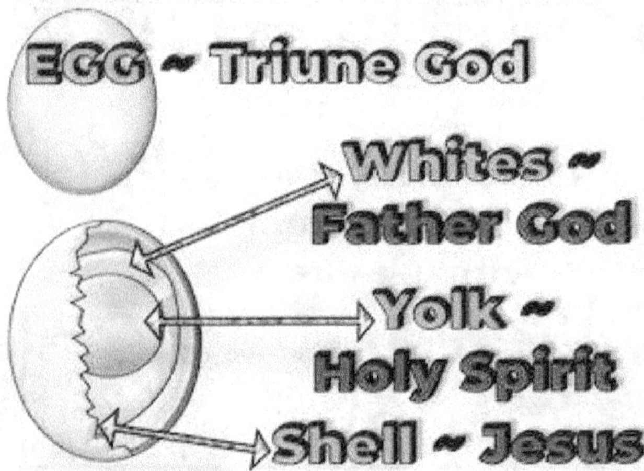

How can we better understand the meaning of the Triune God—God the Father, God the Son, and God the Holy Spirit? Christians and Messianic Jews do not worship three different Gods. We worship one God, which is made up of three parts. To better comprehend this concept, let's use the analogy that the Triune God is like an egg made up of the yolk (i.e., Holy Spirit), the whites (i.e., Almighty God), and the shell (i.e., Jesus who allowed Himself to be cracked open to unveil His Father who surrounds us and the Holy Spirit who lives inside of us.)

Study Guide

Options:
Journal about your Answer.
Pair off to discuss Answers.
Small- or Large-Group Discussion

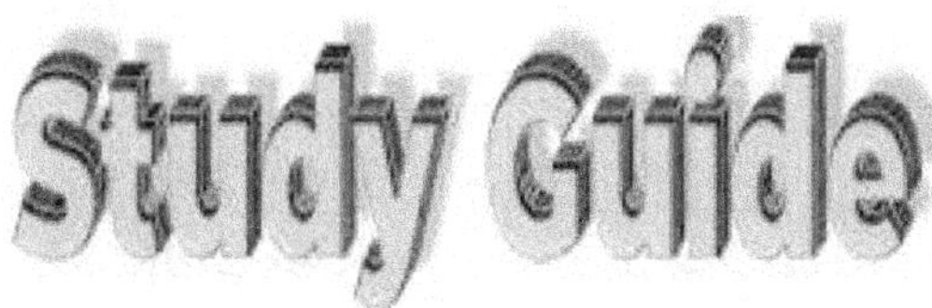

1. What stands out to you about the forty-day period that the Risen Jesus Christ spent with the eleven Disciples?

2. What did you learn about the contents of the Book of Acts?

3. Who did the Disciples choose to replace Judas Iscariot and why?

4. Read this quote about which books of the New Testament were written by Apostle Paul of Tarsus. What do you know about how Paul came to be one of the Apostles?

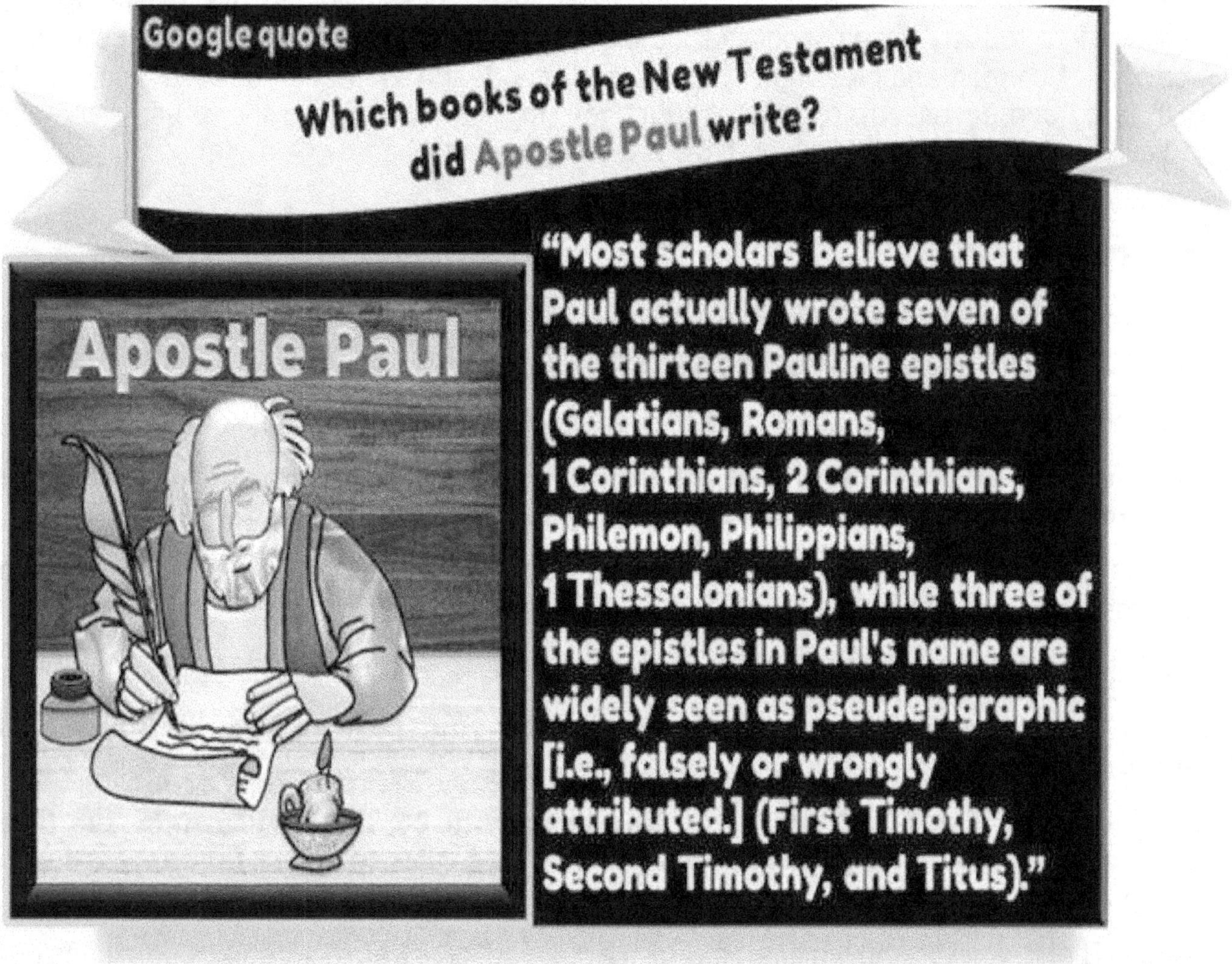
Google quote
Which books of the New Testament did Apostle Paul write?
Apostle Paul
"Most scholars believe that Paul actually wrote seven of the thirteen Pauline epistles (Galatians, Romans, 1 Corinthians, 2 Corinthians, Philemon, Philippians, 1 Thessalonians), while three of the epistles in Paul's name are widely seen as pseudepigraphic [i.e., falsely or wrongly attributed.] (First Timothy, Second Timothy, and Titus)."

5. Look at the list of the seven attributes of the Holy Spirit as described by the Prophet Isaiah. Which one or ones are most meaningful in your life? Please explain.

Author's Dedication

There are many ways to demonstrate our love for and worship of our Lord Jesus Christ. This book is a rendering of data points for you to prayerfully consider that might give your worship of Him a deeper dimension. I dedicate this book to all honest seekers of truth. May it provide another viewing point of the **WORD** in the Holy Bible.

Author's Acknowledgements

There was a deeper purpose for authoring this book. I wrote this book not for my glory but for the glory of our Heavenly God the Father, God the Son, and God the Holy Spirit. I am so grateful for all the manifold ways God, the **Trinity of three Persons**, continually blesses my life. May this book bless your life, as well.

I acknowledge and am so grateful for all the people who created the Bible APPS, Google, Microsoft PowerPoint, Microsoft Word, the Paint APP, books, videos, movies, talks, and sermons that fed my imagination and blessed my life. I also acknowledge the countless moments of comfort and blessings I receive from my dear and treasured family and friends (both living and deceased), of which I count you, my readers, among them. I am eternally grateful! God bless you all! May you have a blessed and touched-by-God life!

Final Blessings

I find myself speculating if God planted me exactly where He did and gave me all the experiences that He gave me just so I could write this book.

And then I feel the **Holy Spirit** nudging me, reminding me of this Bible verse:

Romans 8:28 And we know that all things work together for good to them that love God, to them who are called according to his purpose. (KJV)

May the **Holy Spirit** touch and bless you, as well, and help you to fulfill the mission that God has prescribed just for you.

I end this book with two final blessings, one by King David, the other by Moses.

Psalm 121:8 The Lord keeps watch over you as you come and go, both now and forever. (NLT)

Numbers 6:24 The LORD bless you and keep you. 25 The LORD make his face shine upon you and be gracious to you. 26 The LORD turn his face toward you and give you peace. (NIV)

AMEN. Thank you for making the time to read a part or all of this book. Kindly consider leaving a review, even if it is only a sentence or two.

Also, if you found it pleasing, please share this book with the people you love.

BIBLIOGRAPHY

Bibliography: Used for entire book

Bible Gateway.com. (October 2023 to April 2024). Read the Bible. Website; https://www.biblegateway.com/

Developer Unknown. (October 2023 to April 2024). Bible – Daily Bible Verse KJV. From a free cell phone APP.

Google.com Search Engine. (October 2023 to April 2024).

Grammarly.com for editing (October 2023 to April 2024).

Kairos Software LLC. Developer. (October 2023 to April 2024). Bible KJV Strong's Concordance. From a free cell phone APP. (October – November 2023)

On-line dictionary via Google Search Engine. (October 2023 to April 2024).

Bibliography: Resources to increase my understanding

Barker, Margaret for Marquette.edu. (March 2024). Beyond the Veil of the Temple. The High Priestly Origin of the Apocalypses. Website: https://www.marquette.edu/maqom/veil.html

Bible info.com. (March 2024). Was Jesus in the tomb for three days and three nights? Website: https://www.bibleinfo.com/en/questions/jesus-in-tomb-for-three-days-nights

Brindle, Wayne for Liberty University (March 2024). The Census and Quirinius: Luke 2:2. Website: https://digitalcommons.liberty.edu/cgi/viewcontent.cgi?article=1072&context=sor_fac_pubs

Brownell, Dan. (November 2023). Jesus in the Old Testament. Website: https://pointmetojesus.com/jesus-in-the-old-testament/

Daily Prayers.org. (March 2024). Fate Of The Twelve Apostles & Matthias. Website: https://www.daily-prayers.org/jesus-life-stories-2/fate-of-the-twelve-apostles-matthias/

Fruchtenbaum, Arnold for Jews for Jesus.org. (March 2024). The Messianic Time Table According to Daniel the Prophet. Website: https://jewsforjesus.org/learn/the-messianic-time-table-according-to-daniel-the-prophet

Got Questions.org. (November 2023). Did Jesus go to hell between His death and resurrection? Website: https://www.gotquestions.org/did-Jesus-go-to-hell.html

Heinrich, Bill for Mysteries of the Messiah.net. (March 2024). 04.03.09 Bethlehem (c. 6-5 B.C.) The Registration or (Census). Website: https://www.mysteriesofthemessiah.net/2016/01/04-03-09-bethlehem-c-6-5-b-c-the-registration-or-census/

Henrickson, Rev. Charles. (December 2023). "Not One of His Bones Will Be Broken" (John 19:31-37). Website: https://stmatthewbt.org/2016/03/25/not-one-of-his-bones-will-be-broken-john-1931-37/

Hunt, Michal for Agape Bible Study.com. (March 2024). PLAN OF THE TABERNACLE. Website: https://www.agapebiblestudy.com/charts/Plan%20of%20the%20Tabernacle.htm

Kantor, Mattis for Chabad.org. (November 2023). Timeline of Jewish History. Website: https://www.chabad.org/library/article_cdo/aid/3915966/jewish/Timeline-of-Jewish-History.htm

Ligonier.org for Ligonier Ministries. (April 2024). Firstfruits and Pentecost. Website: https://www.ligonier.org/learn/devotionals/firstfruits-and-pentecost

Ligonier.org for Ligonier Ministries. (April 2024). The Importance of Pentecost. Website: https://www.ligonier.org/learn/devotionals/importance-pentecost

Passion for Truth Ministries on YouTube. (April 2024). The Connection to Passover to Pentecost - Jim Staley. Website: https://youtu.be/1_1uj6EX1co?si=-ivCqj2cIKJSdiSb

Pastor Karla. (December 2023). Jesus Rides Into Jerusalem on a Colt That Has Never Been Ridden. Website: https://pastorkarlablog.wordpress.com/2018/03/25/jesus-rides-into-jerusalem-on-a-colt-that-has-never-been-ridden/

Revealed Truth.com. (March 2024). Where Did Jesus Go When He Died? Website: https://www.revealedtruth.com/bible-study/where-did-jesus-go/

Robinson, Robert, Clifton. (November 2023). What Happened to Our Sins When Jesus Died? Website: https://robertcliftonrobinson.com/2014/09/06/what-happened-to-our-sins-when-jesus-died/

Slick, Matt for Carm.org. (March 2024). What is the Holy of Holies? Website: https://carm.org/other-questions/what-is-the-holy-of-holies/

Stucki, Joel. (April 2024). Why the Resurrection Is More Than You May Think It Is. Website: https://openthebible.org/article/why-the-resurrection-is-more-than-you-may-think-it-is/

The Bible Study.co.uk. (December 2023). Bible History – Making a Timeline. Website: https://thebiblestudy.co.uk/articles/bible-history-making-a-timeline/

Understand Christianity.com. (February 2024). Chronology of Jesus' Life and Ministry. Website: https://www.understandchristianity.com/timelines/chronology-jesus-life-ministry/

Wikipedia.org. (March 2024). John the Apostle. Website: https://en.wikipedia.org/wiki/John_the_Apostle

Wikipedia.org. (March 2024). Judas Iscariot. Website: https://en.wikipedia.org/wiki/Judas_Iscariot

Wikipedia.org. (November 2023). Mary Magdalene. Website: https://en.wikipedia.org/wiki/Mary_Magdalene

Wikipedia.org. (March 2024). Matthias the Apostle. Website: https://en.wikipedia.org/wiki/Matthias_the_Apostle

Wilson, Larry W. for Wake-up.org. (November 2023). The Mystery of Mary Magdalene. Website: https://wake-up.org/bible-characters/mary-magdalene-mystery.html